W9-DAE-603

Cover art by Donna Currier

This book is dedicated to the spinning wheel craftsmen of the past. Their work remains for all of us to learn from.

Interweave Press
306 N. Washington Ave.
Loveland, CO 80537

ISBN #0-934026-04-1
Library of Congress Card Catalog Number 81-80903
First printing: 3M:481:JL
Second printing: 3M:184:JL
Third printing: 3M:586:JL
Fourth printing: 3M:989:JL

Foreword

If you bought this book to learn how to spin, forget it!

If you are thinking about buying a spinning wheel and you're not sure what to look for, or if you have a spinning wheel that doesn't work right, or you're running into problems building your own spinning wheel, congratulations—you're in the right place!

The aim of this book is to answer questions about spinning wheels and their operation, construction, repair, restoration, maintenance and transportation. I will tell you how to evaluate a spinning wheel's condition, how to make simple repairs, and how to be sure that the spinning wheel you're building will work properly. I will help you take proper care of your spinning wheel and I will tell you how to transport it safely.

To put it simply, this is a spinning wheel "buyer's guide" and "owner's manual".

Introduction

People often ask, "What got you started?" Basically, it was an interest in crafts coupled with a desire to do something different, something no one else did. I was doing a lot of crocheting, so why not make my own yarn? Also, I had always been fascinated by spinning wheels in museums and storybooks; I could see how the treadle worked the wheel and the wheel worked "something else", but where did the yarn go? As the old saying goes, "Curiosity killed the cat, satisfaction brought it back." So I learned to spin. And that was just the beginning.

I have a strong aptitude for anything mechanical, so it was very natural to go from using spinning wheels to repairing them. Once I understood how a spinning wheel worked, I could look at a wheel and tell what was missing and why it wasn't doing what it should. I won't say that I can diagnose *any* spinning wheel, but I have had only one so far that had me completely stumped.

This started out to be strictly my project, but whenever I ran into problems I would turn to my dad, and it soon became a partnership. I come from a long line of German craftsmen. My dad is a tool and die maker by profession and one of the best woodworkers that I know. He's taught me a lot about woodworking and I've taught him a lot about spinning wheels, and between the two of us there has been nothing (so far) that we couldn't fix. Although I will admit that there have been some rather hopeless looking spinning wheels brought to us.

This book is an outgrowth of my repair work, and also of several years' teaching spinning and lecturing on spinning wheels. I have seen so-called "working" wheels for sale that weren't worth a darn, and have had people bring these spinning wheels to me wanting to know why they wouldn't work and what could be done about it. People have come up to me at classes and demonstrations to tell me about how their spinning wheel wasn't working right and they didn't know what to do about it. I have had people ask me to look at an antique spinning wheel that they were considering buying because they weren't sure if it was worth the price being asked. And I've seen spinners struggling with stiff wheels, slipping bands or loose parts because they didn't know how to correct these problems.

There are many fine books on the market that will teach you how to spin, but very little to tell you how to evaluate a spinning wheel, how to maintain it and how to make simple repairs. Also, what information there is contains a good many contradictions, not to mention some misinformation. And I have yet to find a good "how-to" book on spinning wheel repair.

So this is (I hope) the answer to the questions, the solution to the problems, and advice for those who don't know what to do.

Happy spinning.

Acknowledgements

I would like to thank my late great-grandfather Emil Alwin Pauli, a master craftsman and perfectionist who left behind many fine tools and an impossible set of standards, and my father Birt Jordan Pauli, who taught me how to use these tools and how to "do the job right!", and who served as my technical proofreader.

I would also like to thank whichever member of the Joliet Weaver's Guild called me up three days before the 1976 Midwest Weaver's Conference to ask, "Could you do a workshop on the care and feeding of spinning wheels?" and thus provided me with both the idea and the title for this book.

Table of Contents

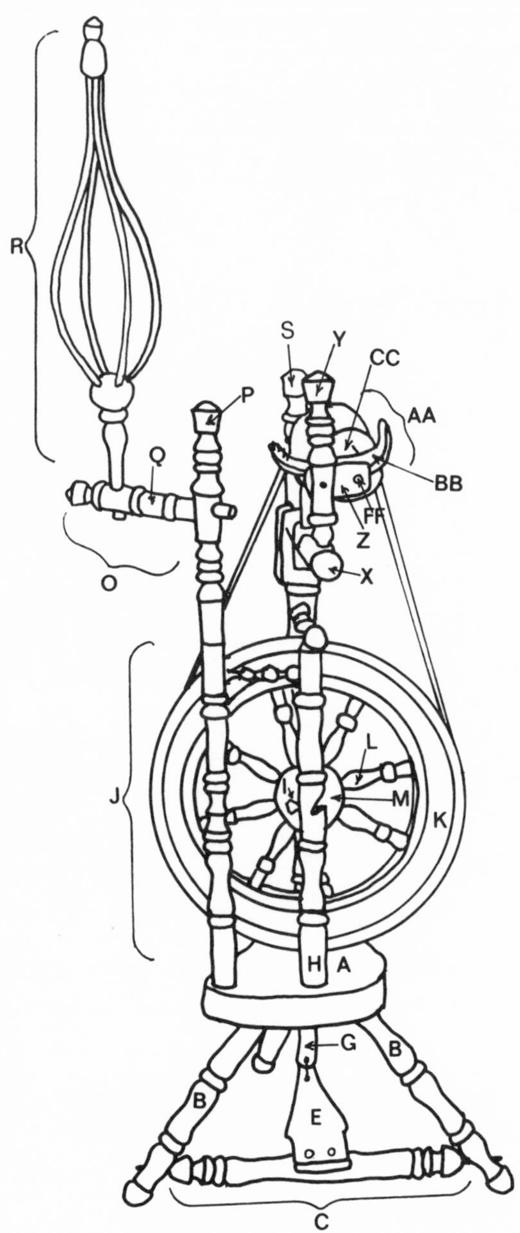

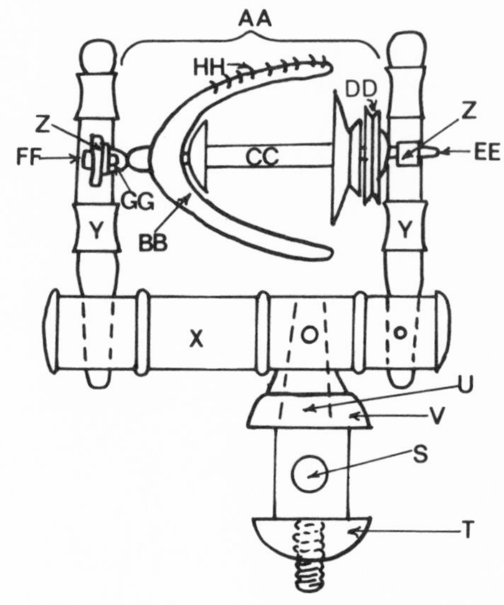

A bench
B legs
C treadle
D pivot bar*
E footboard*
F back bar*
G footman
H wheel posts
I wheel pegs
J wheel
K rim
L spokes
M hub
N wheel crank (back view)
O distaff holder
P upright*
Q cross arm*
R distaff
S tension screw
T locking nut
U spinning assembly support post*
V collar
W drive band
X mother-of-all
Y maidens
Z leather bearings

AA spinning assembly
BB flyer
CC bobbin
DD flyer pulley
EE shaft
FF orifice
GG exit hole
HH hooks

**my own name for this part*

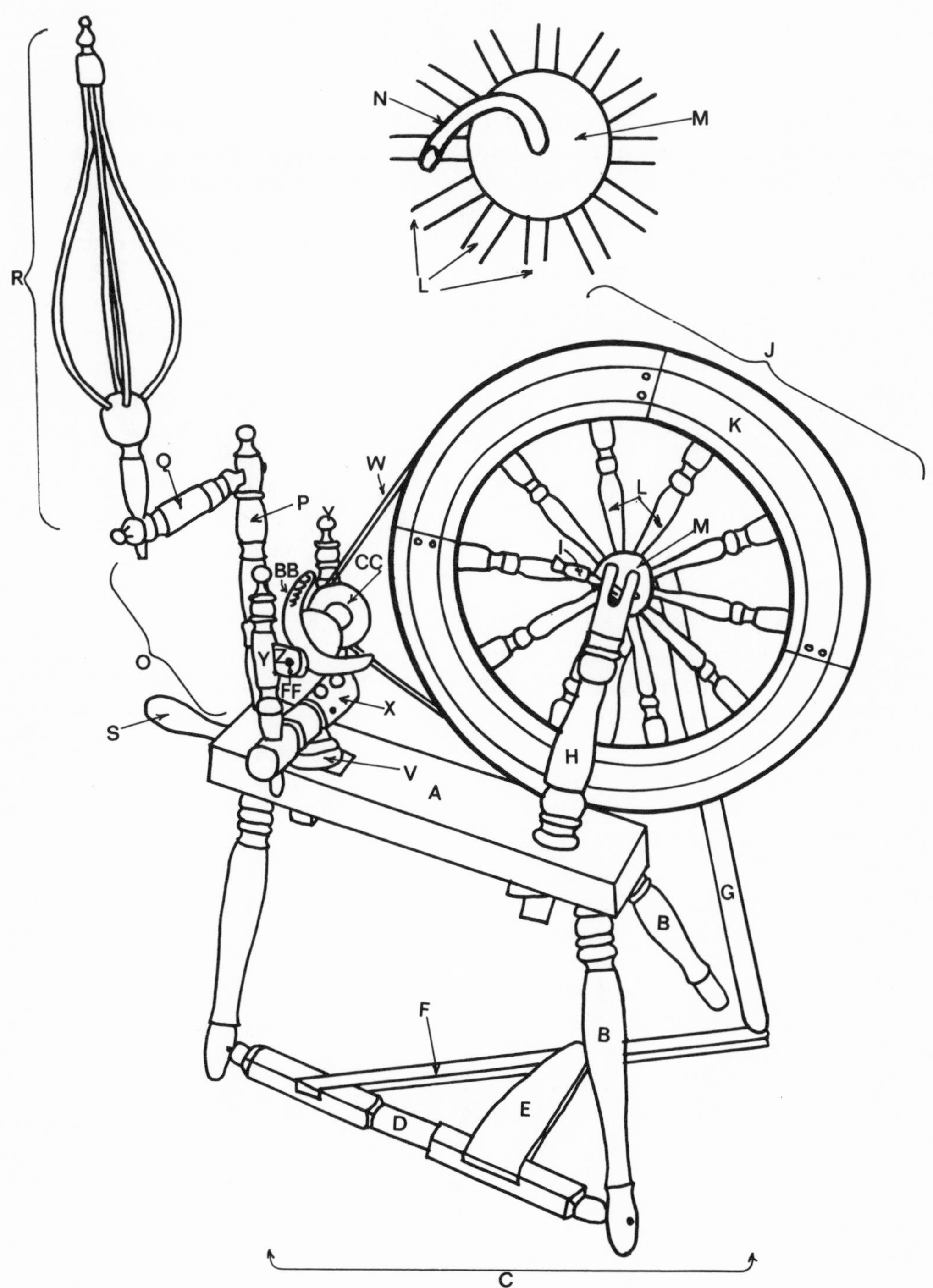
R
N
M
L
J
K
O
P
Y
W
L
M
I
BB
CC
Y
Z
FF
O
X
S
V
A
H
G
B
F
B
E
D
C

GLOSSARY

Allen Wrench. A rod of hexagon shaped metal bent into an "L" shape. Fits into a hexagon shaped hole in the head of allen head screws and is used to turn them. Also called a hex wrench.

Bar Clamp. A clamping mechanism attached to a metal bar or pipe of varying length. Used to clamp large items together while glue dries. Also known as a pipe clamp.

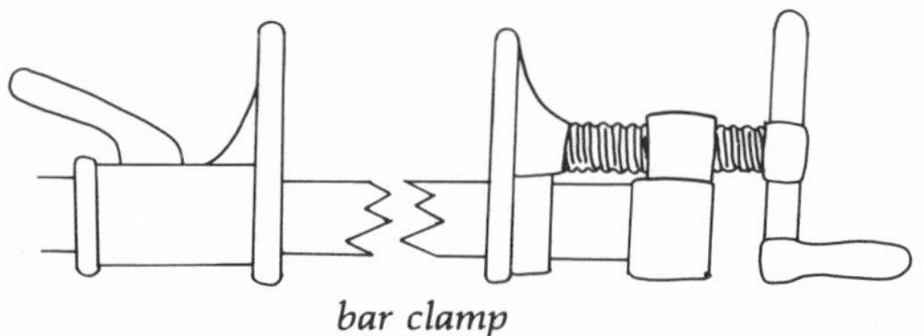

bar clamp

Braze. To fasten pieces of metal together by melting brass brazing rod with a torch.

C Clamp. A screw-operated clamp shaped like a "C". Comes in sizes from about 1" (2.5cm) to about 10" or 12". They are measured by the maximum thickness that they will clamp.

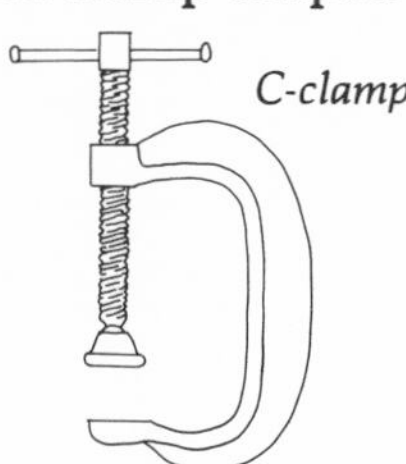

C-clamp

Chuck. A unit consisting of three or four jaws that are expanded or brought together by turning a ring or key, and which grasp an item. On a drill, this is the part that grasps the drill bit.

Coping Saw. Hand-held saw using a "C" shaped frame to hold a narrow blade. Used for making cuts that must curve or turn a corner.

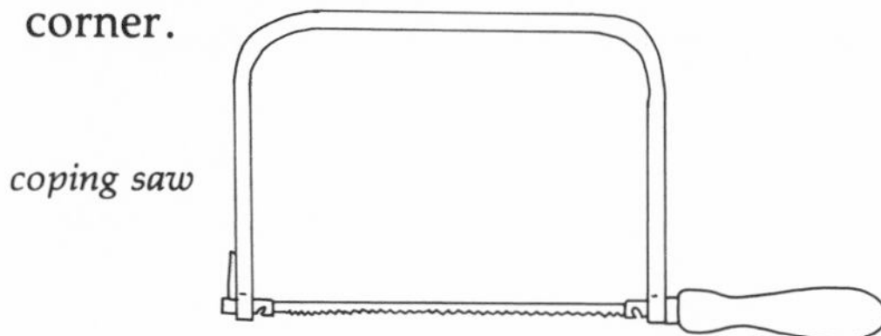

coping saw

Dowel Rod. A round wooden rod, usually birch or maple. Comes in fractional size diameters from 1/8" (approx. 3mm) to 1½" (approx. 3.8cm).

Drill Press. A power drill in a floor or bench stand that can be lowered and raised by a lever to drill holes in materials held on a table attached to the stand.

Epoxy Cement. An extremely strong type of cement. It comes in two parts, resin and hardener, which are mixed in equal amounts. It comes in clear, opaque, quick setting, steel filler, putty form and others. To epoxy something is to adhere it using epoxy cement.

Finger Clamp. A clamp consisting of a wooden "finger" screwed down to a base

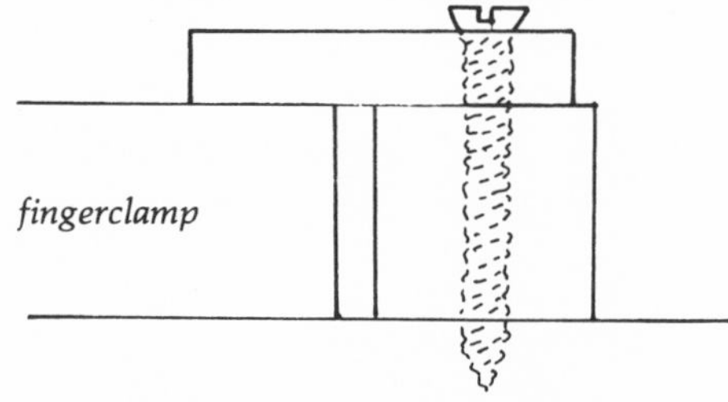

fingerclamp

the same height or slightly shorter than the piece being clamped. It's used to hold items down while they are being worked.

Finial. A decorative knob on the end of a post. On a spinning wheel these are sometimes made out of "ivory" (bone).

Grain. The direction the wood fibers lie in a piece of wood. "With the grain" means parallel to the fibers; "against the grain" means perpendicular to the fibers.

Hardwood. Wood from a tree that sheds its leaves in the fall. Maple, birch, ash, cherry, walnut, oak, etc.

Jig Saw (also called a scroll saw). A power saw having a narrow blade and used for cutting curved lines. Jigsaw puzzles were originally made of thin wood and cut on a jig saw.

Lathe. A power tool which holds a piece of wood or other material and spins it at a high speed while a cutting tool is held against the wood to shape it.

Milk Paint. Milk was sometimes used as an adhesive base for early paints. "Barn red" consisted of the most readily available color (red ocher) mixed with leftover milk and painted on the barn. Occasionally also used on spinning wheels.

Peg or **Cross Peg.** To drill a hole where two pieces join and drive a wooden peg in to hold them together.

Ream. To clean out or enlarge a hole by running a tool through it.

Set Screw. A screw threaded into a part and tightened to hold that part on a shaft or axle.

Softwood. In general, wood from trees that stay green year round. Pine, fir, cedar. Not very good for spinning wheels.

Solder. To fasten two pieces of metal together using a low temperature melting alloy (solder) heated by a soldering iron or torch.

Turn. Wood turning. To shape wood on a lathe. (see LATHE)

Warp. 1. In wood, the variation from a plane surface; often occurs with changes in humidity. **2.** The threads used in weaving that are threaded on the loom (noun). **3.** To wind thread onto the warp beam of a loom (verb).

Weft. The threads used in weaving that are sent back and forth through the warp threads.

Weld. To fasten two pieces of metal together by melting (fusing) the edges.

I
WHAT KIND OF WHEEL IS IT?

My first spinning wheel, and still my favorite, is a style known as an upright, or parlor wheel. It's not the typical early American or storybook style. Consequently, I have had many people ask me what it was or what I was doing because they didn't recognize it as a spinning wheel! In olden times, there were almost as many different styles of spinning wheels as there were makers. Everyone had his own idea of what a spinning wheel should look like, and folk art played a big part. But they can be broken down into basic categories and styles, which simplifies things a bit.

SPINDLE WHEELS

In the beginning, there was the spindle, and the spindle begat the spinning wheel. A spindle is a straight shaft, usually of wood, with a disk or weight of some sort to give it momentum (Fig. 1.1). Most often, it hung down from the yarn being formed, or was supported on the ground, and twirled to twist the fibers into yarn, which was then wound onto the shaft of the spindle. For more on spindles, read *Handspindles* by Bette Hochberg (see bibliography).

The first spinning wheel came about when someone mounted a spindle horizontally in a holder and added a wheel to turn it. This goes so far back in history that authorities are not sure exactly where it originated, but are fairly sure that it was either India or China. The Indian Charkah wheel (Fig. 1.2), used primarily for cotton, and its oriental counterpart (Fig. 1.3), used for cotton or silk, are the same today as they were centuries ago. Other examples of these spinning wheels can be seen in *Spinning Wheels, the John Horner Collection.*

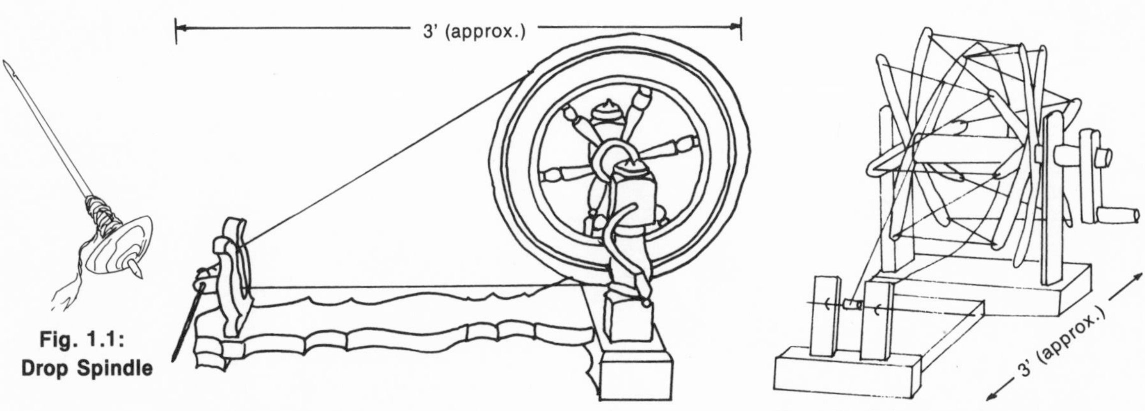

Fig. 1.1: Drop Spindle

Fig. 1.2: Indian Charkah Wheel

Fig. 1.3: Oriental Spindle Wheel

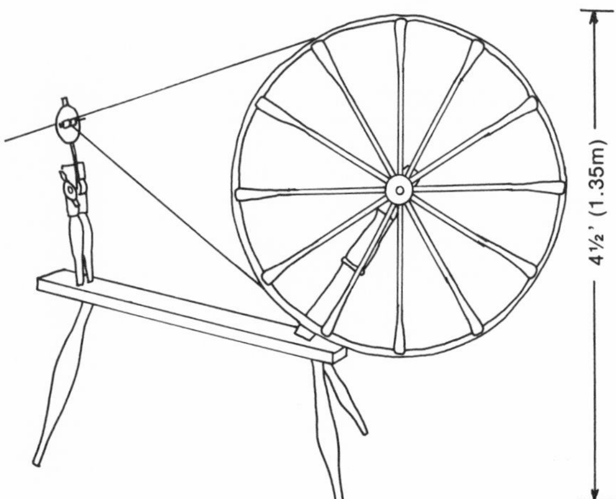

Fig. 1.4: Wool Wheel

WOOL WHEEL

When this design reached Europe, the wheel was greatly enlarged and the whole unit was set up off the floor on legs. This became known as the wool wheel. The spinner would turn the wheel with her right hand while drawing out the fiber with her left, taking several steps backward as she drew out a length of yarn. The wheel was then reversed a short distance to back the yarn off the tip of the spindle, and then turned forward again to wind the thread on near the base of the spindle. The spinner would walk backward as she spun, forward to wind on, backwards again to spin, etc. Thus the wool wheel was also known as the walking wheel. It's also called the high wheel or great wheel, as most of these are 4' to 5' (120cm to 150cm) tall.

The wool wheel (Fig. 1.4) consists of a slanted bench on three legs, two on the low end and one on the high. On the low end there is a single post to hold the wheel. The wheel is fairly simple with an oak band about ¼" (7mm) thick and 2" (5cm) or more wide, bent round while it's green to form the rim. About half of the wheels I've seen have a single groove in the rim; the others are smooth. On the high end of the bench is a tension device (Fig. 1.5) to control the tension on the drive band. Coming up from the tension device is a post holding the spindle head.

There are two basic types of direct drive spindle heads. The bat head (Fig. 1.6) is a flat piece of wood with an area hollowed out to accommodate the spindle pulley. The other style (Fig. 1.7) consists of a cross bar called the "mother-of-all" and two upright posts called the "maidens". (Honest! That's what they're called!) The bearings, which hold the spindle on the maidens,

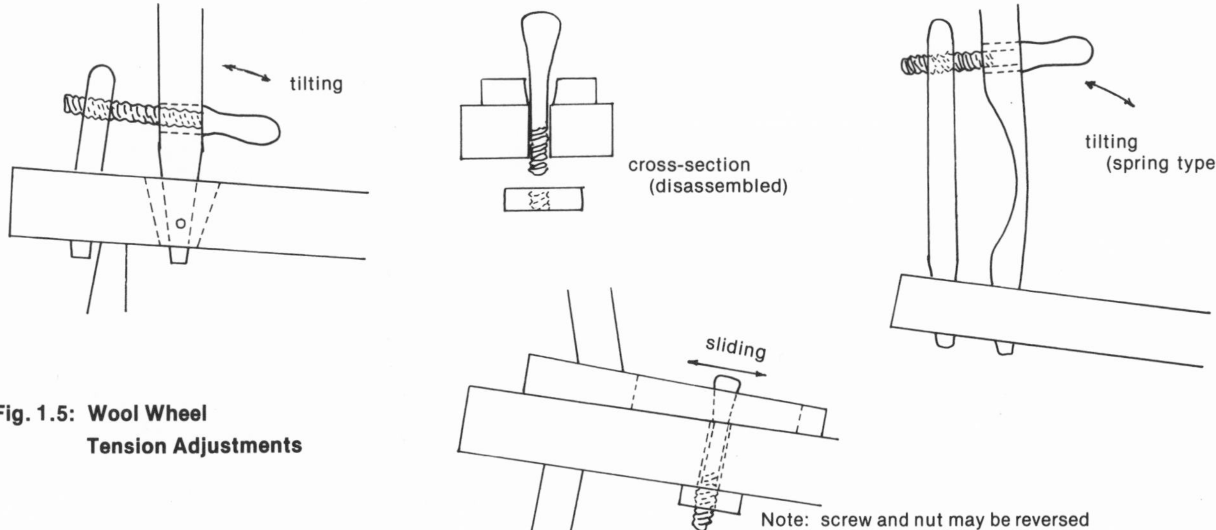

Fig. 1.5: Wool Wheel Tension Adjustments

Fig. 1.6: Bat-head Spindle Head

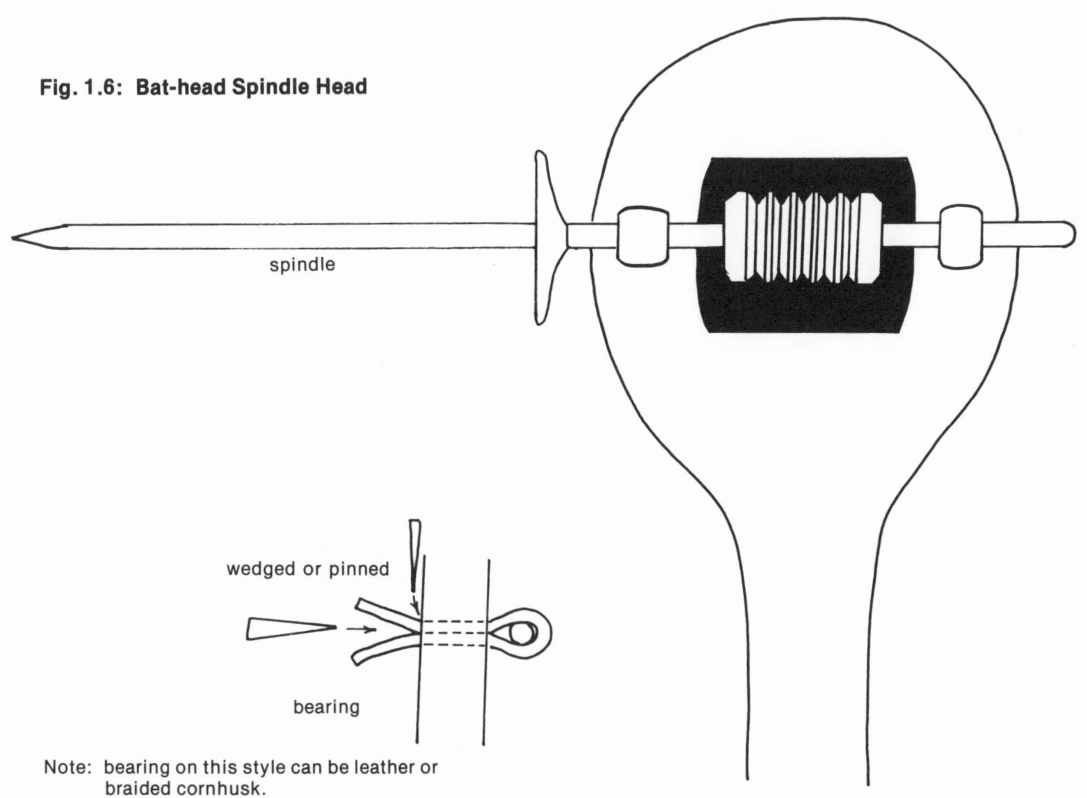

Note: bearing on this style can be leather or braided cornhusk.

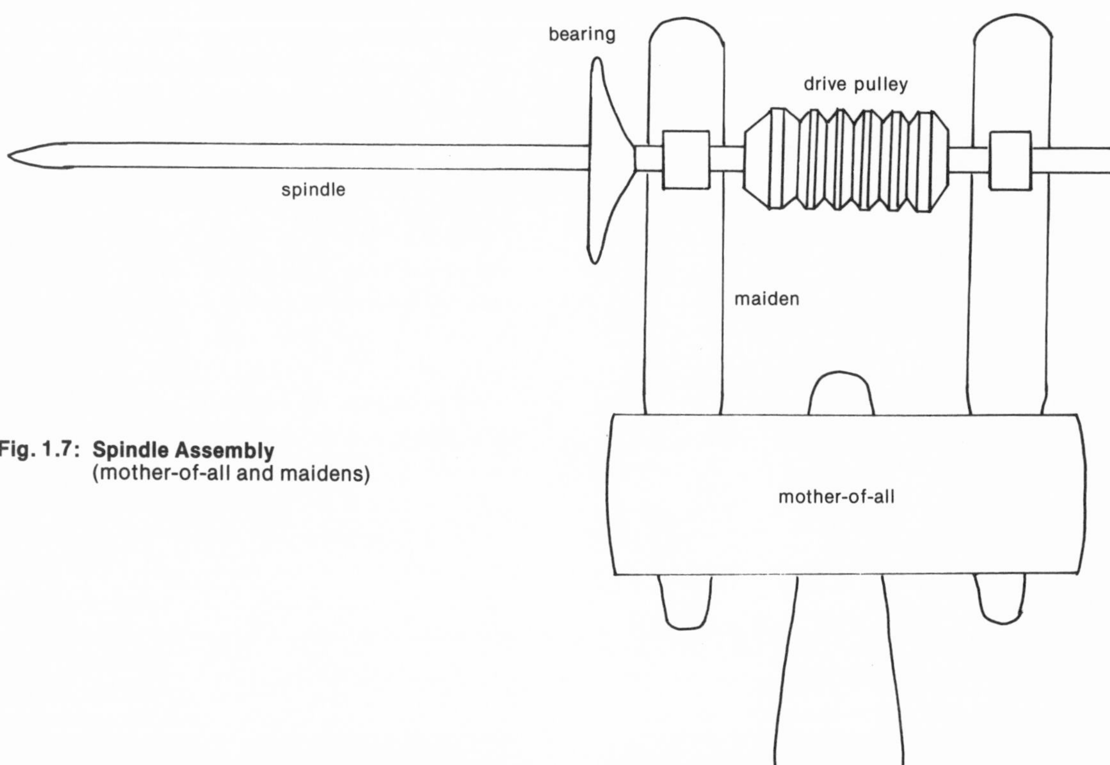

Fig. 1.7: Spindle Assembly
(mother-of-all and maidens)

were usually made of braided corn husk or strips of leather. The spindle itself is a metal rod, pointed on one end, with the pointed end extending out to one side of the spinning wheel.

There is a single drive band going around the wheel, around the spindle pulley, and back to the wheel. It was usually a braided or plied linen or cotton cord, with the ends either spliced or lapped over and sewn together. Turning the wheel (with a finger or a short stick held against a spoke) turns the spindle by means of the drive band.

An improvement, in the form of an accelerating spindle head, was invented and patented by a New Englander named Amos Minor during the early 1800's (Fig. 1.8). This was a spindle head with an additional pulley which was turned by the wheel and in turn ran the spindle. This arrangement gave greater speed to the spindle; it seems to have been very popular judging from the number of them still in existence.

Pendulum Wool Wheel. As with almost everything, you also have "Yankee ingenuity's" attempts to "build a better mouse trap." In other words, some things are so simple and basic that there is no way that you can improve on them, but people try anyway. Such a case is the pendulum wool wheel (Fig. 1.9), patented by L. Wight in the year 1856.

The purpose of the pendulum wheel was to allow the spinner to sit down while she worked and move the spindle away from

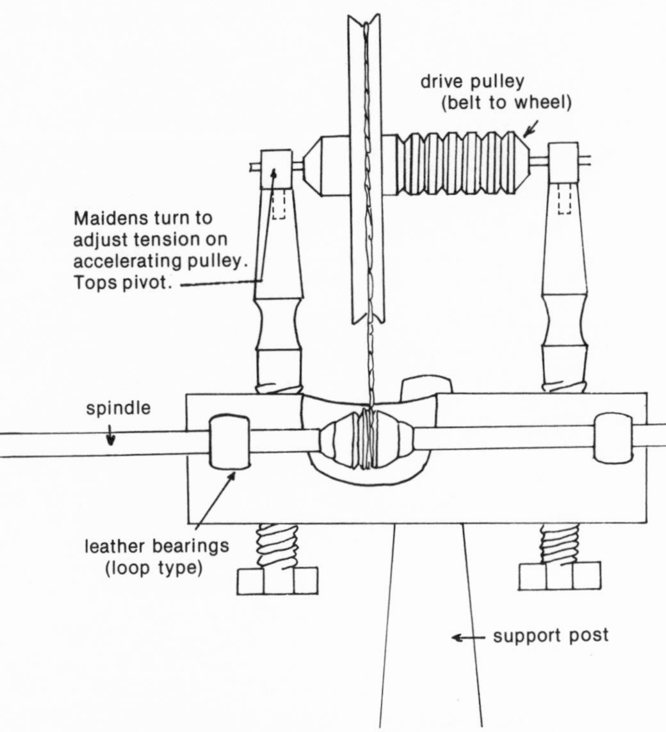

Fig. 1.8: Minor's, or Accelerating, Head

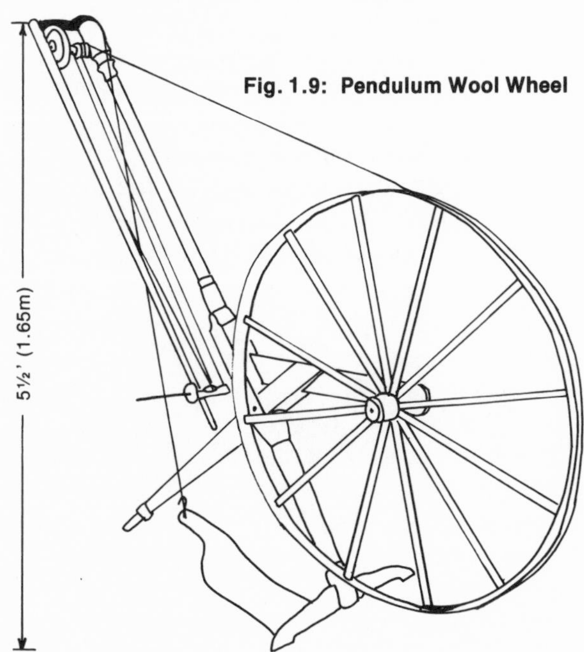

Fig. 1.9: Pendulum Wool Wheel

her instead of her moving away from the spindle. This was accomplished by mounting the spindle at the end of a long pendulum arm which was swung away from the spinner by a foot pedal.

One of these was brought in to us for restoration, missing about half its parts. If it weren't for a photograph in David Pennington's book *A Pictorial Guide To American Spinning Wheels,* I wouldn't have known what we had. As it was, Dad and I had to go up to Octagon House, a museum in Watertown, Wisconsin, and measure and photograph the relatively complete pendulum wheel in their collection, in order to figure out what ours needed. We explained our problem to the museum and they very kindly allowed us to climb over the railing and go into the exhibit. Their wheel was missing the foot pedal, so we had to guestimate from the photo in Pennington's book. Our wheel was also missing the pendulum, and it was too long and narrow for us to try to turn on our lathe. But Dad took a good look at the pendulum on the museum's wheel and thought about it for a bit, and came up with an idea. We bought an inexpensive pool cue and stripped the finish off it. It fit perfectly.

I got to try the pendulum wheel out before it was returned. It takes a little getting used to; you have to be careful that the pendulum doesn't swing back too far and hit you in the face when you let up on the pedal. But basically it works pretty well. Unfortunately it came along a little late in American spinning wheel history to develop a very great following. If you wish to take a first hand look at one you can visit Octagon House Museum in Watertown, Wisconsin; Upper Canada Village in Ontario, Canada; or The Looms at The Brewery in Mineral Point, Wisconsin.

Quill wheels. The wool wheel is nice for spinning a thin, even, traditional yarn, but for a thick or textured yarn you do not have much control as one hand is occupied with turning the wheel. To overcome this problem, a treadle operated spindle wheel has been devised. Originally patented and manufactured under the name Penguin Quill (Fig. 1.10), this was a simple, efficient, well built wheel resembling the bird it was named after. It consists of a two-footed base with a treadle, and an upright post supporting the wheel and spindle. The wheel is a solid disk of wood, as is the spindle pulley. The spindle pulley has a rubber edge and the wheel turns the spindle by direct contact, eliminating the need for a drive band.

When the Penguin Quill first came out it was an immediate success. It is still available from one supplier, as are several other versions under different trade names.

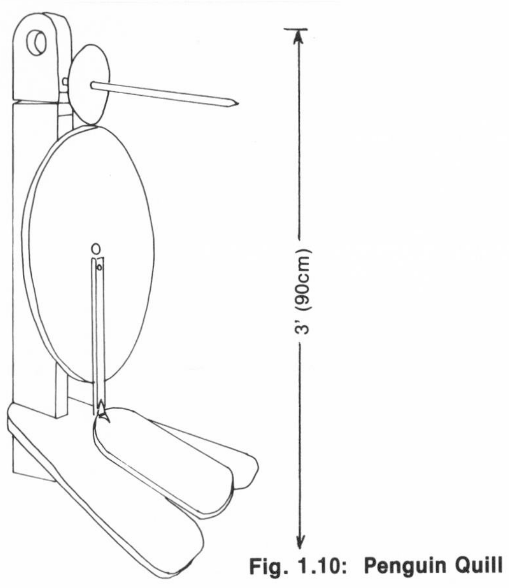

Fig. 1.10: Penguin Quill

SPINNING ASSEMBLIES

No matter what form the spindle wheel took, it still required the spinner to perform two separate operations — spinning and winding. Eventually, people felt that "there's got to be an easier way" and the spinning assembly was born. Leonardo da Vinci worked on the problem, as can be seen in collections of his notes and drawings. A woodcarver named Johan Jurgen from Bremen, Germany, is credited with inventing the double-pulley spinning assembly in 1530. But by then its time had come and it was no doubt "invented" in several places in Europe, which would account for two variations on this device that are also in use. These three are known as the double-pulley, the bobbin lead and the flyer-lead.

Double-pulley. Basically, the spinning assembly is a small mechanism that spins and winds at the same time. The double-pulley, or Jurgen's spinning assembly, is the one commonly found on most spinning wheels, old or new. It consists of a metal axle shaft, with a "head" on one end having a hole called the "orifice going in the end and exit holes coming out the sides. If this sounds confusing, take a look at the diagram (Fig. 1.11). Mounted on the shaft is a "U" shaped piece of wood called the flyer,

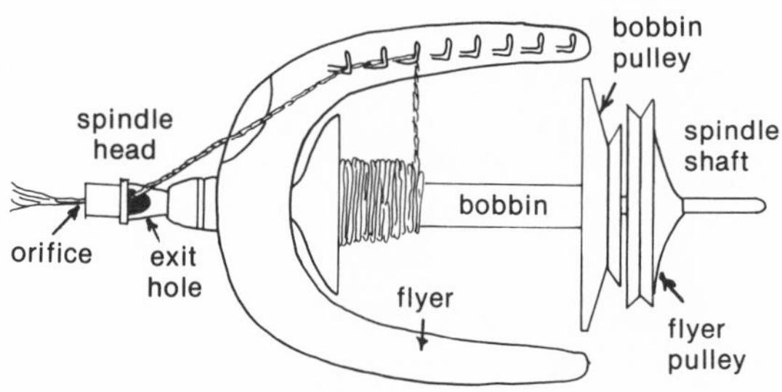

Fig. 1.11: Double Pulley
(Jurgen's spinning assembly, traditional)

with hooks along the arms of it. Inside the flyer is a wooden spool called the "bobbin", which has a pulley at one end. There is another pulley after the bobbin, which usually screws onto the shaft with a left-handed* thread.

As a rule of thumb, the circumference of the bobbin pulley groove should measure at least one quarter smaller than the circumference of the flyer pulley. In other words, if the flyer pulley groove measures X, the bobbin pulley groove must measure X-¼X or less. This means that the flyer turns at one speed twisting the fibers into thread, and the bobbin turns faster and draws the thread in and winds it on. The thread goes in the orifice, out the exit hole, along the arm of the flyer and through the hooks, and onto the bobbin.

Bobbin-lead. The bobbin-lead spinning assembly (Fig. 1.12) is found on some types of older spinning wheels. It is basically the

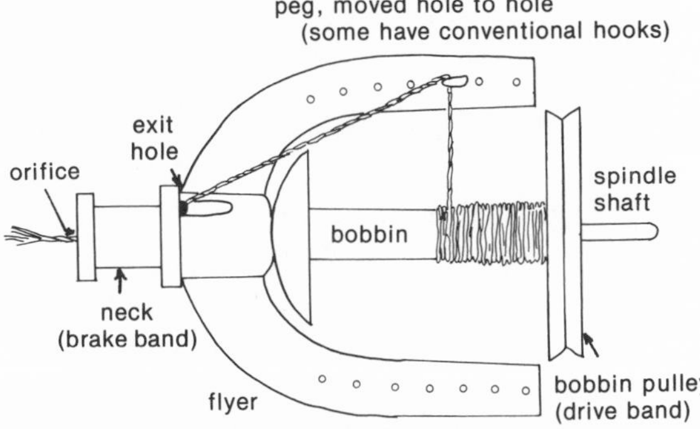

Fig. 1.12: Bobbin Lead Spinning Assembly
(Swiss—some Tyrolean)

same as the double-pulley except that it has no flyer pulley. Instead it has a brake band running (usually) across the head of the shaft. The principle behind this type is that the flyer isn't driven directly by the drive wheel; rather it is pulled around by the yarn in phase with the bobbin while spinning is taking place, but slows down or stalls when tension on the yarn is released so that wind-on occurs. One unusual feature that I have noticed on most of the bobbin-lead spinning assemblies that I have seen so far is that there are no hooks. Instead there is a peg that is moved from hole to hole down the arm of the flyer as the bobbin is filled.

Flyer-lead (sometimes called Scotch-tension). The third and last type of spinning assembly is the flyer-lead (Fig. 1.13), which is basically the reverse of the bobbin lead.

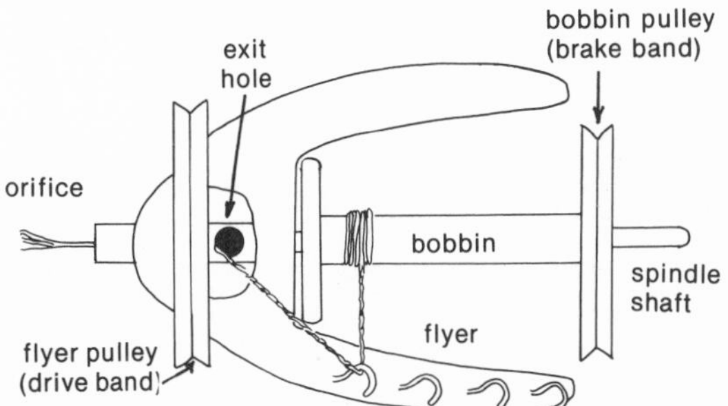

Fig. 1.13: Flyer Lead Spinning Assembly

The flyer is powered and the bobbin is the "follower", slowed by a brake band. But in this case the bobbin is traveling slower than the flyer, and the flyer is twisting the thread and winding it around the bobbin. The most common example of this type is the modern Ashford wheel, which is described later in this chapter.

Double groove pulleys. Some double-pulley spinning assemblies have two grooves in the flyer pulley, one deeper than the other. Folk wisdom is that the deeper groove produces more twist to make a tighter, stronger thread suitable for warp thread in weaving, while the shallower

*Screws backward to the way nuts and bolts, jar lids, etc. turn.

groove provides less twist for a looser, softer thread suitable for weft. Quite logically, these have been called the warp and weft grooves. The two grooves can be used to expand the useful range of the wheel in other ways as well—spin singles on the lesser groove, ply on the greater, etc. On the bobbin-lead spinning assembly the flyer brake band is used to create more or less twist. For the Ashford flyer-lead assembly, a second smaller pulley can be attached to the side of the flyer pulley to give a warp groove, or the brake band on the bobbin can be loosened.

SPINNING ASSEMBLY WHEELS

About the same time as the spinning assembly was invented, someone came up with the idea of the treadle, and the "modern" spinning wheel was born. This type of spinning wheel has not changed from the time of its invention until the recent revival of the interest in spinning. However, the styles vary greatly between geographic locations and ethnic groups. I will attempt to familiarize you with the more common or distinctive styles.

Saxony wheel. The Saxony, or flax wheel, is the most common type, both in Europe and America. The basic overall appearance is like the wool wheel in that it has a slanted three-legged bench with the wheel at one end and the spinning assembly and the tension device at the other. The big difference is in size, about 2′ to 3′ (approx. 60cm to 90cm) tall, which is why it was also known as the low wheel as opposed to the high or great (wool) wheel. It also differs in the addition of a treadle, which earns it the name of flax wheel because the treadle freed both hands to work the long flax fibers. Because this type of wheel was much used for flax, some of them had a flax holder called the distaff.

Although the basic arrangement of the Saxony wheel stays the same, the woodworking styles are as varied as the people who build them. The English Saxonies are fairly large and simple in woodworking style. These, of course, prominently influenced early American spinning wheels (Fig. 1.14). French Saxony wheels have about the same size and proportions as the English wheels, but the wood turning is more delicate and graceful (Fig. 1.15). In

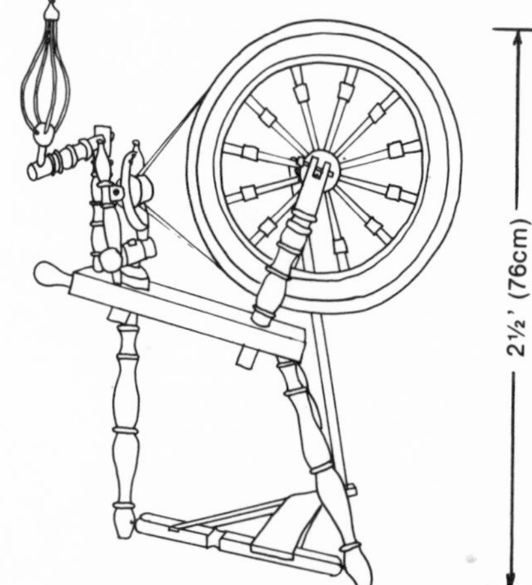

Fig. 1.14: Early American Saxony with Birdcage Distaff

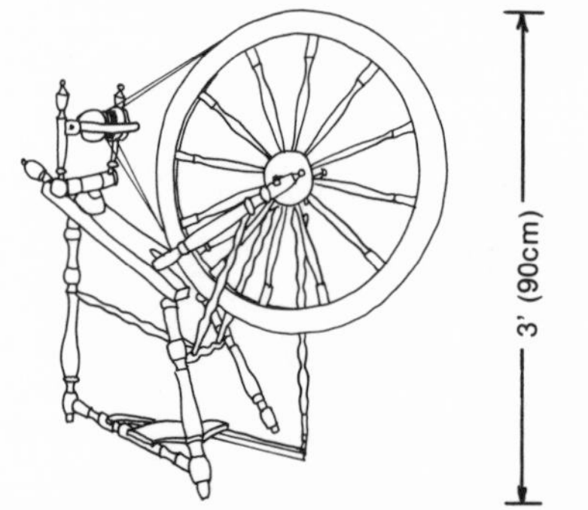

Fig. 1.15: French (or French-Canadian) Saxony (distaff missing)

Germany the wheel becomes smaller and the woodworking more elaborate, while the Dutch put such a thick rim on the wheel that the spokes are often little more than a couple of inches long. As you go further east in Europe the wheels become smaller and the benches more slanted, and the overall effect is that of something out of a fairytale (Fig. 1.16).

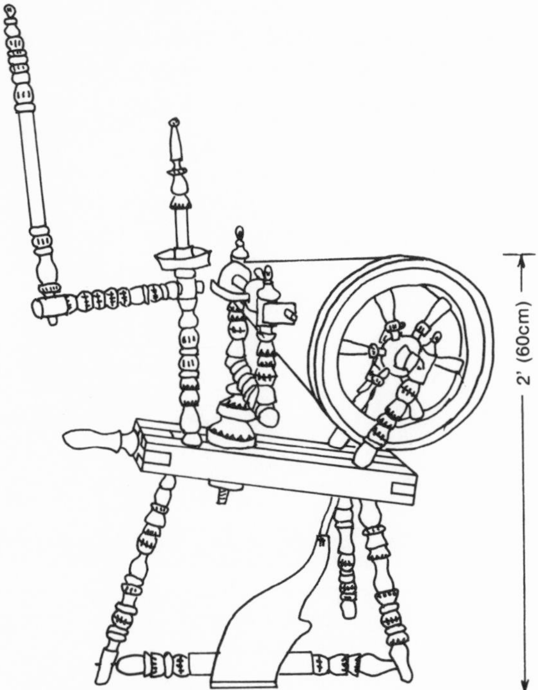

Fig. 1.16: East European Saxony
(with pole distaff and water cup)

Parlor wheel. The second most common type of spinning wheel is known as the parlor, Saxony upright, cottage, visiting, vertical or German wheel (Fig. 1.17). It is basically a compact up-and-down version of the Saxony wheel, and is much more common to central Europe than to America. It has a small stool-like base with at least two upright posts supporting the wheel and above it the spinning assembly. The great advantages to this spinning wheel are its compactness and portability. The one disadvantage is the small wheel; the smaller the wheel, the faster you have to treadle. Some people don't like the uprights for this reason, but I'm rather fond of them.

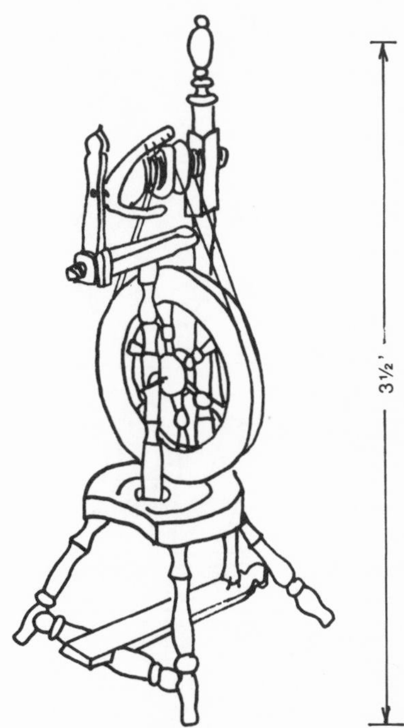

Fig. 1.17: Bavarian Upright

Tyrolean wheel. A third type of spinning wheel that I have been seeing more and more is the Tyrolean (Fig. 1.18). This wheel is strictly European, coming from southern France, southern Switzerland, northern Italy, Austria and points east. The basic design is a rectangular frame base with four legs coming up from this supporting a second rectangular frame. The wheel rests inside one end of the upper frame with the spinning assembly at the other end of the frame. About half the spinning wheels of this type that I have seen have the double-pulley spinning assembly and the other half have the bobbin-lead. I own a rather primitive example which I think may be northern Italian or Austrian. It has the treadle hinged at the side rather than in the front.

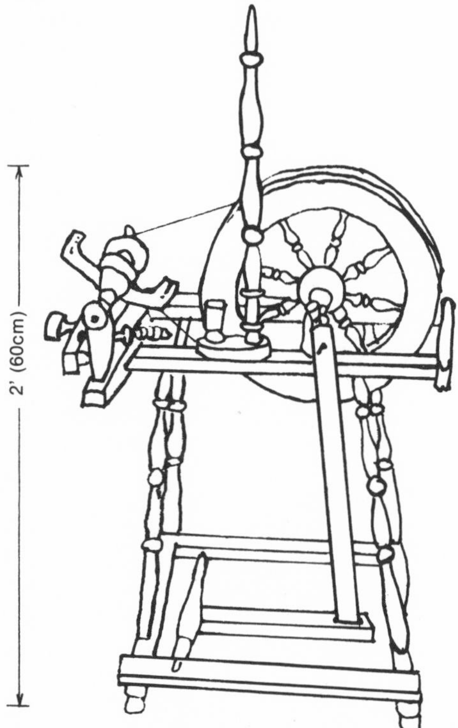

Fig. 1.18: Tyrolean (part of distaff missing)

Treadling is accomplished by resting your heel on the front bar of the lower frame and your toe on the treadle. I have also had the privilege of working on a beautiful little Tyrolean which is allegedly 300 years old from St. Tropez, France. As a four-footed spinning wheel will not always stand as steady as a three-legged wheel will, one of the feet on this spinning wheel is a wooden screw, which for obvious reasons is known as the leveler. This is a rather unique feature which I have seen on only a few spinning wheels.

The above are the three most common types of spinning assembly wheels. However, some areas and ethnic groups have spinning wheels distinctive enough to be classified by themselves.

Irish castle wheel. The parlor wheel is often confused with the Irish castle wheel (Fig. 1.19) because the two both have an up-and-down shape. But the Irish castle wheel has the wheel above the spinning assembly instead of below it. It has three tall legs supporting everything and no bench to speak of. So many people call the parlor wheel a "castle wheel" that I've given up trying to correct them.

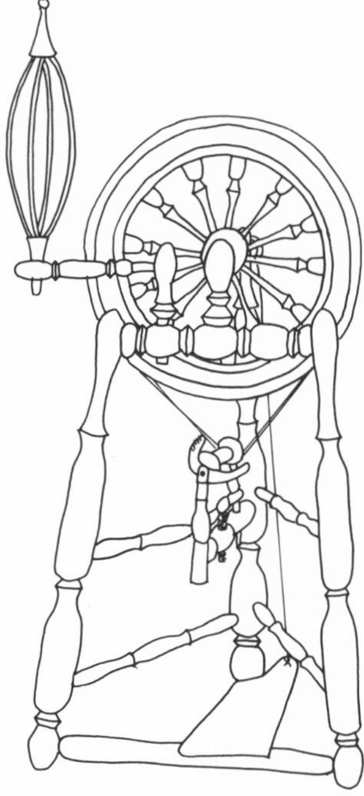

Fig. 1.19: Irish Castle Wheel

Norwegian wheel. Another unique spinning wheel is the Norwegian wheel (Fig. 1.20). It resembles the Saxony in that the wheel and the spinning assembly are side by side on a long, three-legged bench,

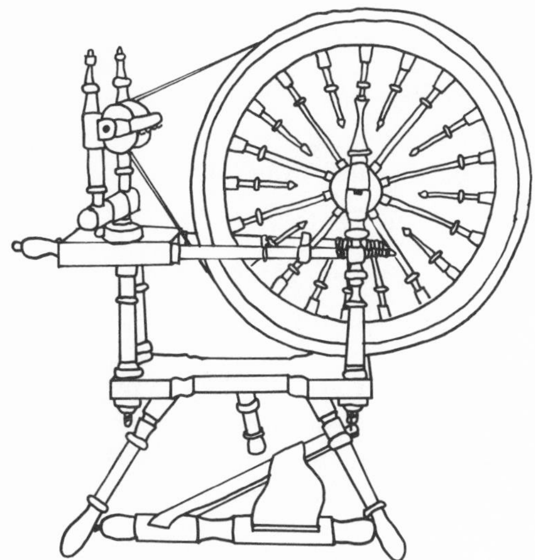

Fig. 1.20: Norwegian Wheel

but there the similarity ends. The bench is level and often rather low. The spinning assembly is mounted up on a platform of its own. The wheel posts are perfectly vertical and are linked to the spinning assembly platform by crossbraces. These crossbraces are threaded and can be rotated to move the wheel posts up and back and thereby bring the wheel into proper alignment with the spinning assembly.

This is a very lovely type of spinning wheel, sometimes very ornate, but without the "chunky" look of some German spinning wheels. Of course, its size may account for that. The Norwegian is one of the largest of the spinning assembly wheels, usually at least three feet tall. I saw one antique in which this ethnic style was combined with another Norwegian art, rosemaling (flower painting). Beautiful! Nice modern replicas of this style are made by Haldane, Steven Gray, Paragon Wheels and others.

Swiss wheel (Fig. 1.21). A rather unusual type of spinning wheel I don't think you'll run into very often, but that I feel is worth mentioning anyhow, is the Swiss wheel. This spinning wheel is an upright with the spinning assembly above the wheel. What's

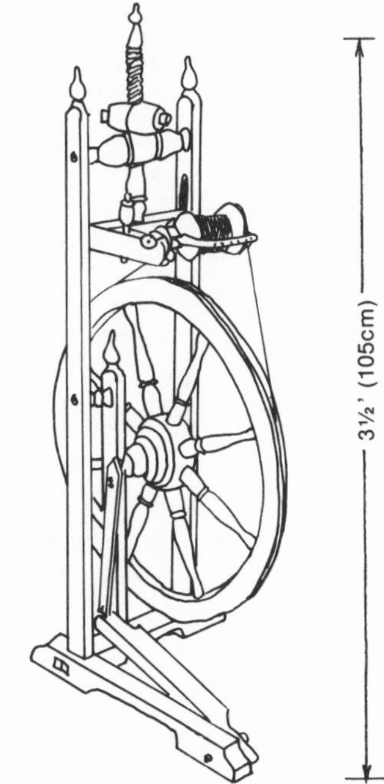

Fig. 1.21: Swiss Upright

really unusual is that the spinning assembly and the treadle are at right angles to each other in such a way that you have to put the spinning assembly sideways to you and feed the yarn in from the left. My own Swiss wheel is pictured in this book. A slightly different example of this wheel can be seen at Miles Mountain Musical Museum in Eureka Springs, Arkansas. Although the styles are slightly different, both spinning wheels function the same way.

Gossip wheel. Another rather uncommon type of spinning wheel is called the gossip wheel. This spinning wheel's origin isn't definitely known. It is usually an upright wheel, but I know of two examples which are Saxonies. What's so different about this wheel is the fact that it has *two* spinning assemblies. It was originally designed for one person to spin with both hands at once. The name "gossip wheel" (also "lover's wheel") comes from the belief that two people could use it to spin at the same time. But this doesn't work very well because different people spin at different speeds and have to stop at different times. A very pretty example of this type of spinning wheel can be seen at Silver Dollar City near Branson, Missouri.

Chair wheel. With the spinning assembly wheels, as with the wool wheel, you find "Yankee ingenuity" attempts to "build a better mousetrap". They are too numerous and varied to list here, but I'll mention the most common type, the chair wheel. It gets its name from its chair-like framework—two short legs in the front and two taller legs/posts in the back connected with crossbraces. This spinning wheel, however, has *two* drive wheels and *two* treadles. The treadles work in opposition to each other, much like pedaling a bicycle, to turn one wheel. This wheel turns the second wheel in an accelerating wheel arrangement. I think that this was supposed to provide a smoother movement. If the drive bands are properly adjusted, it works rather well. I saw a nice example at Smith's Cove restoration in Monroe, New York. Several are also pictured in *A Pictorial Guide to American Spinning Wheels.*

With the recently revived interest in spinning, there is an increasing demand for spinning wheels. There are not enough working antique spinning wheels to fill this demand, and many people don't want to be bothered fussing with an antique. The answer to this is to get a modern built spinning wheel. These generally fall into two categories: replicas and modern wheels. Replicas are new copies of antique spinning wheels, and are sometimes built more for appearance than efficiency, although some of the finest new wheels are replicas. The modern wheels, as I shall call them, place function over form. Many modern wheels are not at all what you would expect a spinning wheel to look like.

REPLICAS

A spinner who wants a "parlor piece" that is attractive to look at or a museum that wants a spinning wheel to use in demonstrations will usually go with this type of wheel. It also seems to be a favorite with the modern craftsmen who produce hand-built spinning wheels.

There are about an equal number of Saxony wheels and parlor wheels on the market, and about four or five wool wheels that I know of. There are even some modern built Tyrolean and Norwegian wheels available. Many of these are pictured in *Spinning and Weaving With Wool* by Paula Simmons. Beware of furniture companies that build replicas chiefly as decorator items. A spinning wheel put out by a spinner or a spinning and weaving supply company is usually a good buy. If you are considering a spinning wheel that is built by a woodworker who is not a spinner or working with a spinner, try it before you buy it or take a spinner along for an opinion.

MODERN WHEELS

These spinning wheels are favored by the production spinner, fiber artist or spinning teacher. Some of them may not be much to look at but they are often more adaptable to a wider range of yarns than the traditional spinning wheels. To keep from turning this book into simply a catalog of spinning wheels, I will mention only a few of the more common or distinctive modern wheels.

Ashford wheel. The most common modern spinning wheel by far is the Ashford wheel from New Zealand (Fig. 1.22). It is very popular with beginning spinners who want a spinning wheel that will work well but won't cost an arm and a leg. The Ashford comes in kit form or ready finished for a little more. It's a simple, well-built little workhorse, plain but graceful and very efficient. It vaguely resembles the Saxony in appearance.

The popularity of this spinning wheel is responsible for a line of accessories, put out by various manufacturers. These include a distaff for spinning flax, a second flyer pulley to give more twist, a spinning assembly with a larger orifice for spinning bulky yarns, and a spindle attachment for converting it from a spinning assembly wheel to a spindle wheel.

Fig. 1.22: Ashford Wheel

I was made sharply aware of the Ashford's great popularity at a spinning workshop that I attended. There were 13 of us in the class; two Saxony wheels, me with my upright, and ten (count 'em, TEN!) Ashford wheels.

Journey wheel. The Journey Wheel is a highly unusual little spinning wheel designed to meet a specific need: portability. The whole spinning wheel folds up into a box measuring 14″ x 16″ x 6½″ (35.56cm x 41cm x 16.51cm) with a leather strap to carry it. Opened, it stands 32″ (81.28cm) tall and has a built-in bobbin holder with two extra bobbins. A rather strange looking spinning wheel, to be sure, but quite practical. A more recent addition to the portable wheel market is the tiny but efficient Louet S-40. Instead of folding into a box like the Journey Wheel, this one has a slipover carrying case and requires very little setup.

Columbine wheel. The Columbine spinning wheel was built for efficiency, not appearance (Fig. 1.23). Nothing could look less like a spinning wheel. The A-frame design is fairly common among modern spinning wheels, but this is the only one made entirely of metal. It has a large comfortable treadle, a double-pulley spinning assembly with a 7¼" (18.4cm) long bobbin and a flyer designed to spin both thick and thin yarn, and nylon bearings throughout the spinning wheel. It's a well built wheel at a low price.

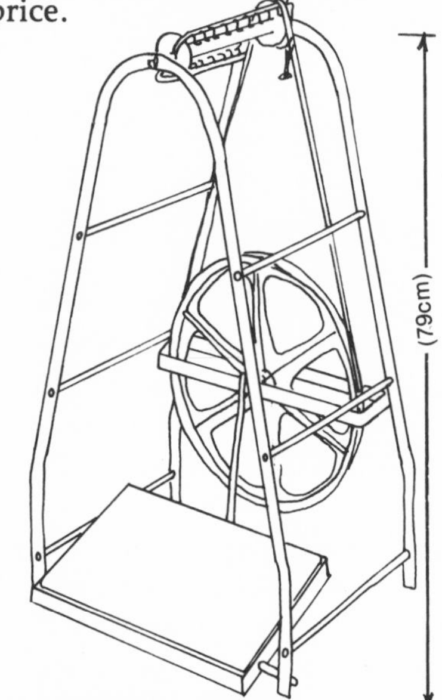

Fig. 1.23: Columbine Wheel

Indian spinner. This is a spinning wheel specifically designed for spinning thick, ropy yarns (Fig. 1.24). There are several models on the market, but all are identifiable by their large spinning assembly (about a foot long) and a large orifice (an inch across). They also have a rather small wheel-to-pulley ratio. The name is derived

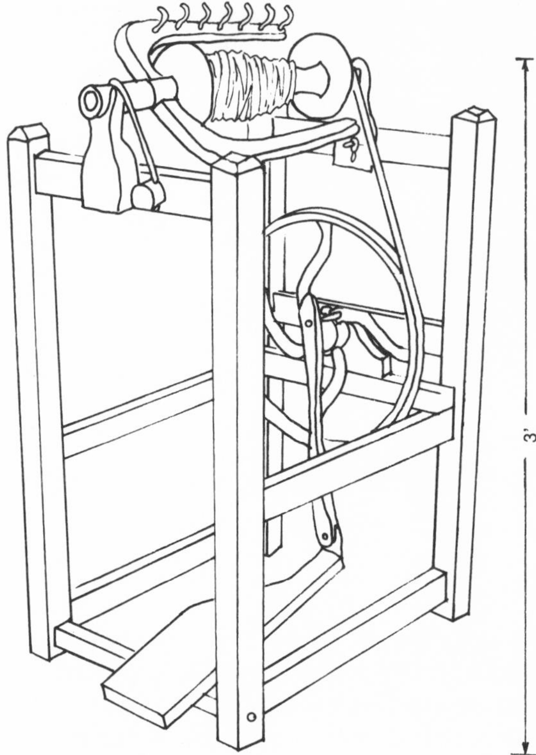

Fig. 1.24: Indian Spinner

from the fact that they supposedly originated with the Northwest American Indians.

THE BEST SPINNING WHEEL

So which spinning wheel is best? A large wheel or a small wheel? A Saxony or an upright? An antique? A reproduction? A modern wheel? The best spinning wheel is simply the one that suits your needs. There is no one spinning wheel that is *the* best for everyone. Some spinning wheels are better for beginners and some are for more advanced spinners. Some spinning wheels are better suited for spinning thick yarns, and some are better for thin, and some are convertible.

The important factors to take into consideration when choosing a spinning wheel are the orifice and hook size (if it is a spinning assembly wheel), the size ratio between the pulleys (if it's a double-pulley spinning assembly), and the size ratio between the drive wheel and the largest pulley (on any spinning wheel). Obviously the orifice should be large enough to accommodate the size yarn you will be spinning. But watch out for wheel makers who "improve" their spinning wheels by making the orifice larger but don't enlarge the exit holes or the hooks. For spinning extra thick yarn the whole spinning assembly should be proportionately larger. And in enlarging the bobbin, it's better to make it longer than larger in diameter. A treadle-operated spindle wheel, of course, will spin any size or texture yarn though not with equal efficiency.

Ratios. Thin yarn requires a greater amount of twist than thick yarn. This means that a spinning wheel designed for thick yarn should have a larger pulley ratio (the size difference between the pulleys) than a spinning wheel designed for thin yarn. Ideally a versatile spinning wheel should have several interchangeable flyer pulleys of different sizes.

To determine the ratio of a double-pulley spinning assembly, measure the circumference of the pulley grooves separately and divide the smaller measurement into the larger one. A 1:1.25 ratio is good for thin yarns; as a general rule of thumb. 1:2 might be more suitable for thick yarn. Any spinning assembly with about 1:1.15 or less won't wind on; to be effective, it should be at least 1:1.20.

The drive wheel to pulley ratio is what determines how fast your spinning wheel goes. To determine the drive ratio, divide the circumference of the larger pulley into the circumference of the drive wheel. A spinning wheel with a low ratio, such as 1:4, is good for a beginner because it can be run very slowly, but it would frustrate an advanced spinner who wishes to produce large amounts of yarn. An advanced spinner would want a spinning wheel with, at the very least, a 1:8 ratio. My upright (1:4) is great for teaching on, but I have to treadle twice as fast as I do with my mom's French Saxony (1:8.75). And in a speed contest such as a sheep-to-shawl competition, an upright like mine would be very impractical unless you want a lot of exercise.

So sit down and decide. What types of yarn interest you? Will you be transporting the spinning wheel a great deal? Do you want something that will look pretty, or simply something that will do the job? Figure out your needs and they will determine the type of spinning wheel that is best for you.

YELLOW PAGES

II
FINDING A SPINNING WHEEL

Deciding what kind of spinning wheel you want is one thing. Finding it is something else. And it can sometimes be rather frustrating. Finding a modern built spinning wheel is no problem; you go to the maker, distributor or retailer and buy one, or you can mail-order. But finding an antique spinning wheel is mostly a matter of being in the right place at the right time. In other words, luck. That doesn't mean that they aren't available, you just have to know where to look.

So where do you look? Everywhere you can. Obviously, the more places you look, the better your chances of finding one.

Antique stores. This is the first place you might think to look, and the best place to find a spinning wheel. However, good spinning wheels sell quickly. They are lovely decor pieces, and now there are a lot more spinners looking, too. If a spinning wheel doesn't sell in a couple of months, it's usually a pile of junk, overpriced or hidden. So as I said, you just have to be in the right place at the right time. If the shop you're at doesn't have a spinning wheel (and they probably won't), talk to the proprietor. Ask if they ever get any spinning wheels in. Some dealers don't want to bother with them, and some will buy up every spinning wheel that they can get their hands on. Find out if they will take your name and phone number and call you if they get a spinning wheel in. The more places that you can leave your name, the better. But don't just sit back and wait for them to call; often they forget. So keep checking.

Checking antique shops gets to be like hunting garage sales. You're driving along and suddenly out of the corner of your eye you spot the sign. You hit the brakes (and hope the car behind you does the same) and take the first turn that will get you back to the shop. Sometimes they're closed, and often they won't have any spinning wheels, but you never know! Once, I took a wrong turn going to a spinning demonstration and went past an antique shop that I wouldn't have found otherwise. I was late, so I couldn't stop then, but I remembered where it was and I stopped on the way home. And so I went home with a lovely Swiss wheel that needed only the finish stripped and a new drive band.

Most of the spinning wheels in my collection have come from antique shops. But not always because I was shopping for a spinning wheel. I just like to prowl antique shops and I'll often leave my business card. One dealer that I visited called me back to say that she had just gotten four spinning wheels in, and would I please come over and sort out the parts and fix them up for her? I ended up buying two of them. One was my mother's French Saxony, which sat in our house for a year waiting for a mail-order part which never came. Mom fell in love with it, so my dad and I bought it from the dealer "unfinished, as is" and fixed it up and gave it to her for Christmas.

The other was a painted Tyrolean wheel that *I* fell in love with.

Antique shows. A good place to look if you don't mind spending some money. Most shows will generally have at least one spinning wheel, but prices tend to run rather high.

Auctions. Estate auctions are generally better than advertised antique auctions. Estate auctions are where the antique dealers get their merchandise and they want to pay as little as possible so that they will make more of a profit. At auctions where you have the general public trying to find some nice antiques for their homes, the bidding will often be higher and you will have more competition. Farm auctions are very good, but not as likely to have spinning wheels. Here are a few helpful rules for auctions:

1. Arrive well before the bidding starts so that you can look the spinning wheel(s) over *thoroughly* beforehand. Is it what you want? How complete is it? How much work will it need? (See next chapter.)
2. Decide what the top price you will go is *and stick to it!* Don't get carried away.
3. I never like to make the first bid. I wait and see how many other people are interested. If no one responds, the auctioneer may come down, or you can make an offer for less.
4. Don't appear too eager, either while examining the spinning wheel or while bidding. If the auctioneer thinks he "has a live one" he'll run the bidding up as high as he can.

Junk shops. By this I mean the enterprise that looks like a cross between a small junk yard and a large garage sale. They buy up overstock, stores going out of business, and miscellaneous estates lock, stock and leftovers. There are sometimes some nice antiques among the junk, and *occasionally* a spinning wheel. You have to keep checking, though. They take your name (sometimes) but they rarely call. The same applies to resale shops.

Want ads. It's a long shot, but you might find a spinning wheel here. I did, once. Dealing with a private party, you will generally run into one of two kinds. They will either want to get rid of "this useless old thing" or they think that they have a Valuable Antique. With the first kind, you can sometimes get a bargain, but they are quite rare. The more common second type will probably be trying for twice as much as the spinning wheel is worth and will turn down any offer you make. Call back in a week or two and they may have come down in price. No? Then re-evaluate. Maybe it's not worth it.

Spinning and weaving supply shops. Although this is more the place to go for new spinning wheels, they might know of a customer with used equipment for sale. Or maybe they'll let you put up a want-ad.

Guilds. If you can contact a spinning or weaving guild, pass the word that you're looking for a spinning wheel. Something might turn up.

PRICES

I can't tell you too much about prices. They vary from place to place and from year to year. Try to get an idea of the price range in your area. Talk to other spinners and to spinning suppliers and antique dealers. Modern spinning wheels range from an Ashford wheel kit for about $100 (at the time of this writing) to well over

$400. Usually, the less you pay the less you get. But there are exceptions. Get a good spinning magazine and go through the ads and send for brochures. As far as antique spinning wheels go, the only price rule seems to be "whatever the traffic will bear". The price will vary greatly based on what the dealer paid for the wheel, the type of shop (junk barn or Antique Shoppe), how fancy the spinning wheel is, and how clean it is. Few antique dealers know how to tell if a spinning wheel works or not so that's not always a cost factor, unless they got it from a spinner and can "guarantee that it works." But you should do your homework (read the next chapter) so that you'll be able to tell. Learn how to evaluate a spinning wheel so that you'll know what repairs it needs. A low-priced spinning wheel is no bargain if the initial cost plus the cost of repairs puts the total above the cost of a more expensive spinning wheel.

So go ahead and start your search. Be thorough and be persistent. And above all, don't get discouraged. It may seem like you're never going to find what you want. And then, when you least expect it, there it is. Two of my spinning wheels were found by serendipity—looking for one thing and finding something else that you're glad you found anyway. I went to an apple orchard that we visit yearly to buy apples and discovered that they had opened an antique shop. I came home with a bushel of apples and a German-American Saxony wheel. At the same time, my parents were on a vacation trip out East. They stopped at an antique shop in Charleston, South Carolina, to look at a yarn winder that was in the window. They came home with the yarn winder and a fancy little East European Saxony that was sitting in a corner of the shop badly in need of tender loving care.

So if at first you don't succeed, don't give up. When I first started spinning, I couldn't find an antique spinning wheel anywhere. Now I own four of them!

III
WILL IT WORK?

All right, suppose you've found a spinning wheel in a shop, or someone has given you one (lucky you!), or you've hauled great-Aunt Fanny's spinning wheel down from the attic. You want to know, "Is it all there?" "Will it work?" For instance, there is someone, somewhere, who is building a very nice looking modern reproduction spinning wheel . . . without a tension adjustment! But it looks pretty and many people don't know the difference! My Swiss upright was just the opposite. It looked like a first-class mess, but was a structurally sound, operating spinning wheel. So here's how to "kick the tires" and avoid getting stuck with a lemon, old or new!

I will use the Saxony wheel as an example in this chapter, as it's the most common type of spinning wheel (Fig. 3.1).

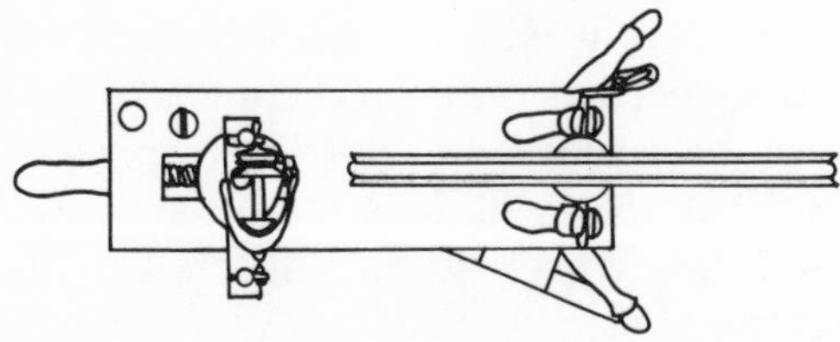

Fig. 3.1: Saxony (top view)

However, the basic information is the same for all spinning wheels. It's also a good idea to refer to the parts identification diagram as you go through the chapter. To start with, you have the bench, or with some spinning wheels a pedestal or framework. It's a thick, wide board that holds all the other parts together. So if the bench is missing, it's rather obvious—you won't have a spinning wheel, you'll have a pile of parts. Changes in humidity can cause wood to expand or shrink; changes are much greater across the grain, so shrinkage often results in cracking or splitting. This kind of problem is fairly simple to fix (see next chapter).

The bench is supported by three, or occasionally four, legs. If any of these are missing you will notice right away. Unless the leg is threaded, anyone handy with a wood lathe can make a replacement. To check if the legs are all original, check the woodturning pattern. The two shorter legs should be identical and the taller leg simply a longer version of the same. Check the wood grain and color. A spinning wheel may be composed of two or more kinds of wood, but the legs should all be the same.

Another problem you may run into is a cracked or broken leg. This means that pressure on the leg or bench has broken the leg across the grain, usually at the bench. Often the spinning wheel has been dropped or bumped or otherwise abused. One customer brought me an upright spinning wheel with two broken legs; one of her kids had used the bench for a footstool! A crosswise break is a serious problem, not for an amateur to repair. It requires a double chuck or machinist's lathe (see Chapter 5, "Professional Repairs"). If you pick the spinning wheel up and the legs fall out, don't worry—they're just loose; remember,

I said that wood shrinks? While checking the legs, feel the bottom of the back leg (the one furthest from you as you face the spinning wheel as you would spin). There was sometimes a metal spike driven into the bottom of the leg to dig into the floor and keep the spinning wheel from creeping away from you as you worked. You will probably want to drive it in or pull it out before you set the spinning wheel down on your good carpeting or no-wax tile.

Between the legs, we come to the treadle. This piece takes a lot of wear, so along with the footman and flyer, it's the most likely to be worn out or broken. The wear on the footboard of the treadle is a good indication of how much use the spinning wheel has had. There are two basic types of treadles. The more common is the pivot bar treadle. This is a solid two- or three-piece treadle that pivots on two metal pins in the ends of the front bar. Some treadles pivot in the middle of the footboard for a heel-and-toe motion similar to a treadle sewing machine. This is rare on antiques, and found mostly on very tiny uprights and some modern spinning wheels. Most treadles pivot at the front (under your heel) for a push-and-coast motion. (See chapter 10.)

The hinged treadle is found on some central European spinning wheels, especially German. It consists of two parts: a stationary front bar fastened to the front legs, and a back bar and footboard fastened to the front bar by leather hinges. Leather dries out and cracks more quickly than wood, so the hinges will probably have to be replaced; but this you can do yourself. Wooden parts that have split or cracked can be glued. Parts that have worn through or broken across the grain will have to be replaced or repaired by a professional.

Going from the treadle to the wheel crank is a "connecting rod" called the footman. This is usually wood, sometimes cord or leather, and often missing from antiques. Anything that wasn't permanently fastened to the spinning wheel is likely to have disappeared, and the footman was fastened to the treadle only by a leather thong. It's not difficult to replace; any good woodworker can make one. Or you can make a temporary one out of string for the purpose of trying the spinning wheel. On a modern spinning wheel check to see that the footman does not hit on anything as the wheel goes around and that it's not so long that the treadle hits the floor.

The footman connects to the wheel, which rests in wheel supports. On the Saxony these are two posts, usually with slots cut in the ends. As with most parts on an antique spinning wheel, you will find that they are a tapered fit in a tapered hole. About half of them will be crosspegged under the bench. Some of them have additional supports and cross-braces. If the post has split at the wheel axle slot, you can glue it. If a piece has broken off completely, you can glue it back on. But if the piece has been lost, you will have to take the post to a spinning wheel restorer and have a new end made for the post.

If you are handed a bundle of parts and told that it's a spinning wheel, you run into the problem of getting the wheel posts into their proper holes. On a new spinning wheel this is not so difficult; just make sure that the slots line up so that the wheel runs easily without binding. On a used spinning wheel or an antique there is a definite right and left. The things to look for are a line or discoloration showing which way they fit in the bench, and wear from the wheel hub rubbing against the side of the axle slot which will help you sort out which goes in which hole. Missing supports or cross-braces can be replaced by a woodworker, and loose posts you can fix yourself.

On an upright spinning wheel, the wheel is supported in slots about halfway up the main posts. These posts also (indirectly) support the spinning assembly. The same problems and procedures apply to the upright as to the Saxony.

Running crossways of the wheel axle slot you will find a hole for a peg to hold the axle down. And with an antique you'll be lucky if the pegs are still in the holes, though they're easy to replace if they aren't. As you are treadling a spinning wheel, you are applying a sharp downward pressure on the back of the wheel axle. This causes the front end to jump around in its slot. And the smaller the wheel, the more it will hop. This causes the wheel to tilt and throw off the drive band. The peg holds the axle down in place and keeps it from jumping. Most all wheels will have a peg in the front post and a fair number of them will also have one in the back, although this is not as important as the front peg. Many Norwegian wheels and a few rare cases of other types have a wooden cap that fits over the end of the wheel post to hold the axle down in place.

Missing pegs are very easy to replace. If the peg is in place and the axle still jumps, either the slot has been worn deep or the peg has been almost worn through. You can fix either problem easily. Occasionally you will find a modern spinning wheel where the pegs are placed too high to do any good. Sometimes these holes can be redrilled. But it should serve as a warning that the wheel maker does not completely understand the operation of the spinning wheel, and the peg placement might not be the only thing wrong with it.

Now we go to one of the two most important items on the spinning wheel, the wheel itself. There are a number of different ways to construct a drive wheel; a typical case might be a rim made up of four sections held together with pegs and/or glue. The number of spokes varies but the spokes are usually fitted into holes in the hub and cut to fit flush with the inside of the wheel rim. The spokes might then be pegged and/or glued to the rim. Check for missing pegs, loose spokes, and gapping joints. And not just on the old wheels; I've seen some poorly built replicas.

If the wheel seems fairly solid, give it a spin with your hand. Stand by the end of the wheel and watch how it runs. This is very important for wool wheels, too. Does the wheel run tilted at an angle? It might be a loose wheel post or a worn axle groove (Fig. 3.2). If there's a problem on a wool wheel, it's probably a bent axle, or the axle hole in the wheel is worn, although some wheels like the Obadiah Tharp are tilted at an angle on purpose. On a new wheel one of the axle grooves is probably too deep or out of line with the other. All of these are fairly simple re-

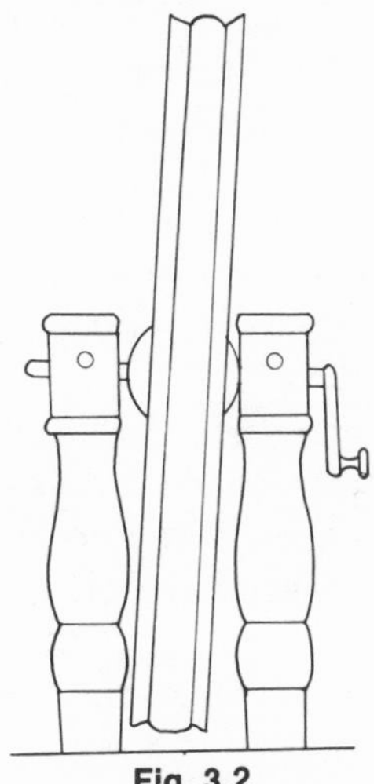

Fig. 3.2
wheel runs crooked
wheel post groove worn

pairs. Does the wheel rock back and forth as it runs? (Fig. 3.3). On almost any spinning assembly wheel this means that the axle is bent (old wheels) or mounted crooked in the hub (some new wheels). Bending an axle back is kind of tricky, but it can be done. Redrilling an axle hole can also be done, but only by someone with a drill jig that will keep the hole perfectly centered and at a perfect right angle to the rest of the wheel.

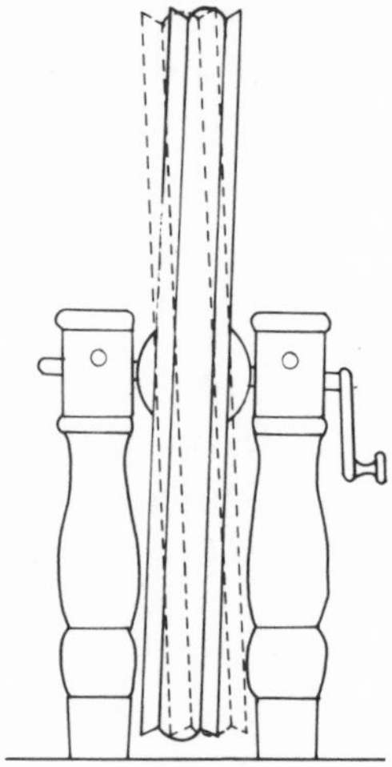

Fig. 3.3
wheel rocks
bent axle

If the wheel has a little wiggle to it as it runs (the axle and hub run steady, but the rim takes a little detour), check the joints (Fig. 3.4). If they're loose, there's your problem; the wheel is falling apart. If the joints are firm and the rim still humps, *look out!* You've got a warped wheel. On a wool wheel, even a small warp can be serious as it's only the perfect lineup of the wheel and the spindle that keeps the drive band in place. On a smaller spinning wheel, constant alignment is not quite as crucial. Important, yes. But the driveband grooves are deeper, so a slight warp will not cause much problem. In fact, I seldom see an antique spinning wheel that doesn't have a slight irregularity. I own one spinning wheel that both humps up and down and wobbles back and forth, but still tracks okay. HOWEVER, if the warp is severe enough to throw the band, *I would pass up this spinning wheel!* There are a couple of methods you can try to straighten a warped rim, but they're not always successful.

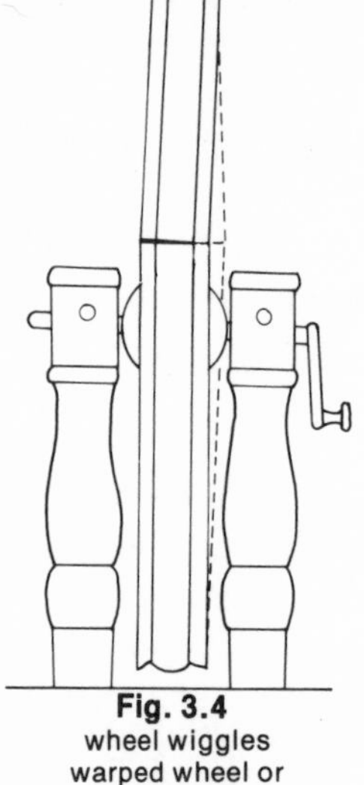

Fig. 3.4
wheel wiggles
warped wheel or
gapping joints

While you're checking the wheel, look at the wheel crank. If it's badly worn, don't worry. It's still quite usable. If it's broken it might be repaired by someone who can solder or weld metal although these methods require considerable heat which could damage the wood. Or a machinist or toolmaker can make you a new one.

Moving now to the other end of the bench, you will often find a handle sticking out of the end. This is part of the tension adjustment, which consists of a wooden screw that slides the spinning assembly holder toward or away from the wheel (Fig. 3.5). It may be stiff, but it should turn. If it won't turn it's probably "frozen" by age, dirt, dried grease, etc. If the weather is very humid, the wood might

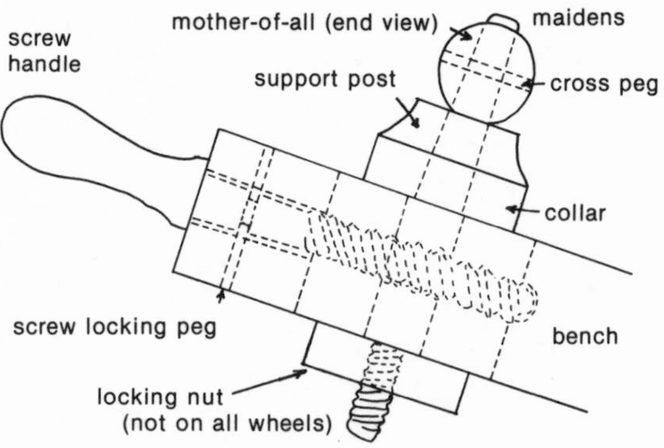

Fig. 3.5: Saxony Wheel Tension Adjustment

have swollen up. And if the spinning wheel was painted or varnished by a latter day owner, the tension screw might have gotten "glued" solid. A liberal soaking of turpentine or paint remover might remedy this. If the screw turns and then binds, either the screw is warped and there is nothing you can do about this short of replacing it, or the wood has aged and shrunken oddly. Rethreading it *may* help. If the threads are stripped from the screw, it will have to be replaced. This can be done by a good woodworker with a set of wood threading tap and dies, or someone who can fit it with a metal screw and nut. Better yet, take it to a reputable spinning wheel restorer. (See Chapter 5, "Professional Repairs".)

Sometimes it is difficult to see the condition of the tension screw because it is hidden inside the bench. On an upright spinning wheel the tension screw may run down the inside of the back support post, turned by a knob or handle at the top (Fig. 3.6). On other upright spinning wheels and on Tyrolean wheels, the tension screw is exposed and can be easily examined (Fig. 3.7). If you can't take the tension adjustment apart, you can judge its condition adequately by feel. One warning: if you can see the tension screw, check for a lot of tiny holes in it. It's strange, but it's been our experience that anytime a spinning wheel has been subject to wood borers or termites, the tension screw usually gets the worst of it. I've seen two spinning wheels where the tension screw handle would twist right off in your hand. And this could be very awkward if the shop's policy is "You break it, you've bought it". An undermined tension screw can be repaired by a spinning wheel restorer, but if you have a choice, I would look for a sounder spinning wheel.

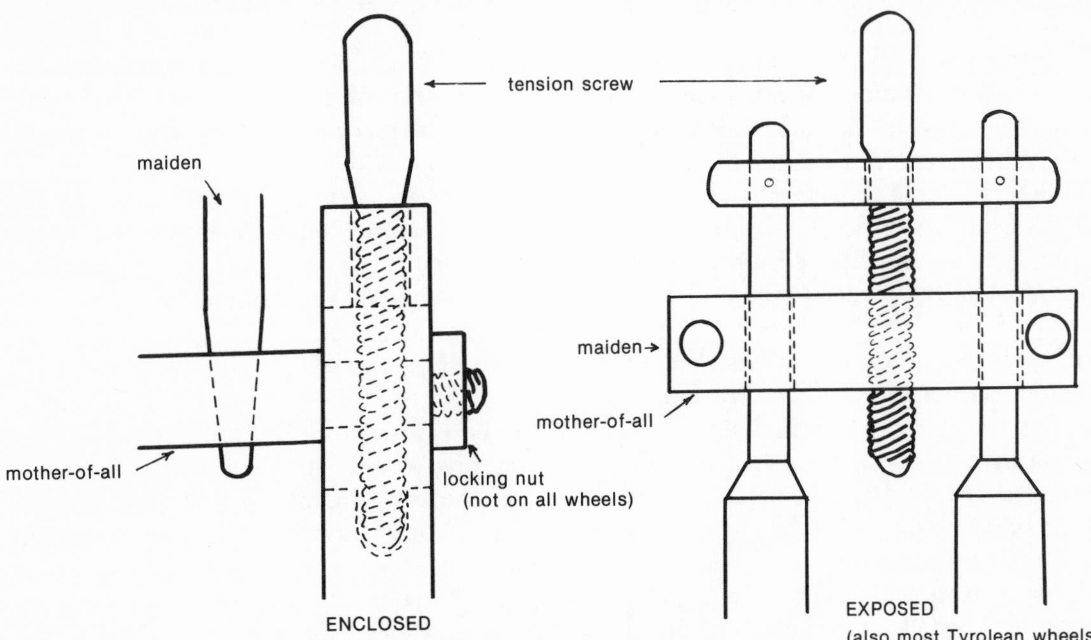

Fig. 3.6 & 3.7: Tension Adjustment, upright wheels

Modern spinning wheels are not immune to tension screw problems, though they generally behave better than antique spinning wheels. A friend of mine bought a modern reproduction upright wheel from a reputable dealer. After using it a bit she told me that she was having problems with it; she couldn't seem to adjust the tension. I took a look at it and discovered that the wooden tension screw handle was not fastened permanently to the metal tension screw. The handle turned, but the screw didn't go anywhere. A little epoxy cement solved the problem.

Sometimes the mother-of-all has a locking nut. On a Saxony wheel this will be located on the underside of the bench. On an upright, it will be on the back of the post. This is loosened before the tension is adjusted and tightened afterward to hold it steady. If the tension adjustment won't move or moves stiffly, check for a locking nut.

The tension screw runs through a piece which I call the spinning assembly support post. This comes up through the bench, through a wooden "doughnut" or collar, and holds a round crossbar called the "mother-of-all". And don't ask me where that piece got its name! The mother-of-all should be securely fastened to the post by a cross-peg. If it's loose, either the peg is missing or broken, or the post has shrunk. No big deal, either way. Replace the peg or shim the post. (See next chapter.)

The mother-of-all supports two upright posts called the "maidens". Occasionally you will find one or both of these missing on an antique spinning wheel. A good woodworker can make a new one. The maidens are usually a tapered fit in a tapered hole, except for the modern spinning wheels which are often a straight fit. The front maiden is often made to turn to release the spinning assembly, but it should stay where it's put and not "wander" during spinning. The back maiden remains stationary and is sometimes cross-pegged, except for the Ashford wheel and antiques where the rear maiden turns and the front maiden doesn't. On some upright spinning wheels the maidens may be horizontal instead of vertical. Or the tension adjustment may take the place of the rear maiden.

The maidens each have a bearing, often leather, to support the spinning assembly. On an antique spinning wheel these bearings may be rather "petrified", in fact they may not resemble leather at all. On modern spinning wheels I have seen everything from nylon to masonite used. I feel, though, that leather is still best. If the leathers are cracked, broken, worn out or missing (on an antique I can almost guarantee it) they are not hard to replace yourself. The front maiden should have a flat slot in it for a flat piece of leather with a hole in it. The back maiden has a hole in it (probably square) for a strip of leather to be doubled over to form a loop. (More on this in the next chapter.)

The wheel itself is one of the two most vital parts of a spinning wheel; the spinning assembly is the other. This little unit does the entire job of twisting and winding the fibers. Without the spinning assembly, the spinning wheel will not work.

If the entire spinning assembly is missing, I would pass up this spinning wheel unless it is very rare or a bargain that you just can't resist. To replace the spinning assembly can be expensive, and you have to take or ship the entire spinning wheel to a spinning wheel restorer. There is only one restorer that I know of who will mail-order this part, and he requires that you make a very detailed set of measurements. Also, you will get a better fit and match if you take the entire spinning wheel to a restorer.

If the spinning assembly is there but parts of it are broken or missing, it's not so bad. Some of this can be handled by a good woodworker (the flyer, hooks, bobbin or flyer pulley), but for a new metal shaft you should go to a restorer, although a good handyman *can* make one. (See Chapter 5, "Professional Repairs".)

On a modern spinning wheel, check to see that the bobbin moves freely inside of the flyer, that the flyer is securely fastened to the shaft, and that the edges of the orifice are smooth so that they won't fray or cut the thread. Also, the bobbin and flyer pulleys must be the correct ratio, 1:1.25 at least, or the yarn will not feed on properly.

The final item on the spinning wheel is the distaff. This is the holder for flax fiber, and the piece most often missing on any spinning wheel. Likewise the distaff holder. Look for a (usually) tapered hole in the high end of the bench on a Saxony, or on a crossarm on an upright wheel, or in the front of the frame on a Tyrolean. The distaff holder sits in this hole and turns to swing the distaff around next to the spinner when she's working with it, or to swing it out of the way when she's not. Because it turned, it was not fastened in and was therefore often lost. The distaff was not fastened in so that it could be removed to be dressed with flax. So you sometimes have a distaff holder but not a distaff, though more often both parts are missing. Also, flax spinning died out before wool spinning did, so many distaffs were no doubt relegated to the attic or fed to the fireplace.

A good woodworker can make these parts for you, but you don't need a distaff if you aren't going to be working with flax. About half of the European spinning wheels didn't have an attached distaff, but used a separate floor-standing distaff. Many modern spinning wheels do not have a distaff because not everyone is into spinning flax. Some wheel makers offer a distaff as an accessory to a spinning wheel and sometimes a distaff made for one spinning wheel can be adapted to another. Modern made floor-standing distaffs are also available.

Looking at the spinning wheel's overall appearance, unless it has been sitting in someone's living room, it will probably not be too clean. Mom's French Saxony was covered with soot when I first saw it. Even if it looks like a first class mess don't worry; all you need are the proper materials and a lot of patience and "elbow grease". If the spinning wheel has been painted or varnished by a latter day owner I would remove the finish. But then, I'm a stickler for authenticity; you can do as you please. If the spinning wheel is Scandinavian, east European or latter day Canadian, the paint is probably original and I would leave well enough alone, except for cleaning. (See Chapter 6, "Restoration".) If you decide to strip the spinning wheel, *please* do it yourself or have it done by a good furniture restorer. *Do not* take it to a "dip stripping" shop, as their methods are too harsh. (More on this later in the book.)

Some modern spinning wheels come unfinished or in kit form. If you're handy with a paint brush, you can have a nicely personalized wheel. You can stain it to match your furniture or paint a design on it. I saw an Ashford wheel with daisies on it; it looked very nice. A friend who does medieval Celtic artwork painted an illuminated manuscript design on her modern replica wheel. I've always wanted to paint an Ashford blue with red Pennsylvania Dutch tulips. With a modern wheel you can do as you please.

SUMMARY

Used spinning wheels. Look for a spinning wheel that has a good solid wheel and spinning assembly. It should be essentially complete, not counting pegs or the distaff. Loose parts are acceptable, but it should be basically sound. Don't worry about how clean it is.

New spinning wheels. A new spinning wheel should be nice and solid. The spinning assembly and the drive wheel should spin freely but not slop around, and they should line up with each other exactly. The treadle should move freely without hitting the floor. The bobbin should move easily within the flyer and the pulleys should be the correct ratio. The orifice should be smooth and large enough for the type of yarn that you will be spinning. Treadling the spinning wheel should give the feeling of a solid, smooth piece of machinery.

Wool wheels. The bench, legs and posts should be sound and the tension adjustment should be complete and working. The wheel must run true! A missing spindle can be replaced, but the spindle head should be intact.

IV
DO-IT-YOURSELF REPAIRS

Now that you know what problems to look for, I'll tell you what to do about them. I'll start with some definitions and some general ground rules.

You will notice that in the last chapter I mentioned three basic categories of people: yourself, a woodworker and a restorer.

1. **Yourself.** I don't know who will read this book so I have to assume that everyone is not mechanically inclined. I refer to the type of person who can handle simple household repairs and has a hammer, a screwdriver and some glue somewhere around the house.

2. **Woodworker.** If your hobby is woodworking and you have a basement or garage workshop with a wood lathe, you belong in this category. Or maybe some member of your family or a friend or neighbor does woodworking. If all else fails, try the woodshop teacher at your local high school. Maybe they, or one of their better students, would be willing to make the needed part(s) for you.

3. **Restorer.** This is a person who makes a specialty of repairing and restoring spinning wheels. See the next chapter and the source list in the back of the book (p. 74).

This chapter will deal with the first two categories; what you can do and how to do it.

GENERAL RULES

1. Never glue anything without clamping it!

2. Use a wood putty (such as Plastic Wood) only as a last resort to fill cracks that can't be drawn together by gluing and clamping.

3. Find an assistant (any pair of hands that can follow directions). This will prevent a lot of frustration when you are trying to do something like hold two pieces together and tighten a clamp at the same time. I started my basement apprenticeship at an early age this way, helping my dad.

4. There is no such thing as standard size replacement parts for antique spinning wheels. Each wheel is unique and all parts must be custom made.

5. Read Chapter 6, "Restoration", before working on an antique spinning wheel.

SOLUTIONS TO SPECIFIC PROBLEMS

Lengthwise cracks and splits. A crack is where, through age or abuse, the wood has started to separate other than at a joint. A split or break is where the two pieces have parted company completely. A split is a separation lengthwise of the grain and will be discussed presently. A break is a crosswise separation and will be covered in the next chapter.

To mend a crack or split, you will need one or more C or pipe clamps big enough to hold the piece, and something to pad the clamps so that you won't mar the piece that you are gluing. You can use scraps of wood, heavy cardboard or rag. You will also need a good polyvinylacetate resin ("white") glue or aliphatic resin ("yellow") glue especially for wood, such as TiteBond or Wilhold. I strongly recommend dry clamping; that is, clamping without glue first (Fig. 4.1). This will show you if the piece will be drawn up all the way, or if the clamps will slip, or if you will need more clamps. An assistant to hold the padding in place while you tighten the clamps (or vice-versa) is very helpful. When you are satisfied with the clamping arrangement, remove the clamps and get the glue.

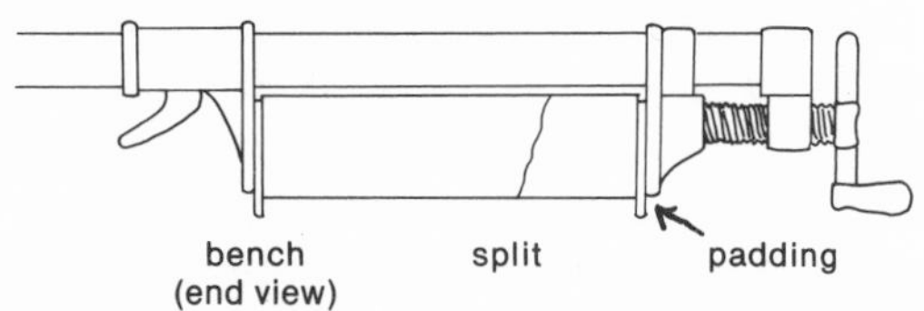

Fig. 4.1: Glueing a split or crack using a pipe clamp

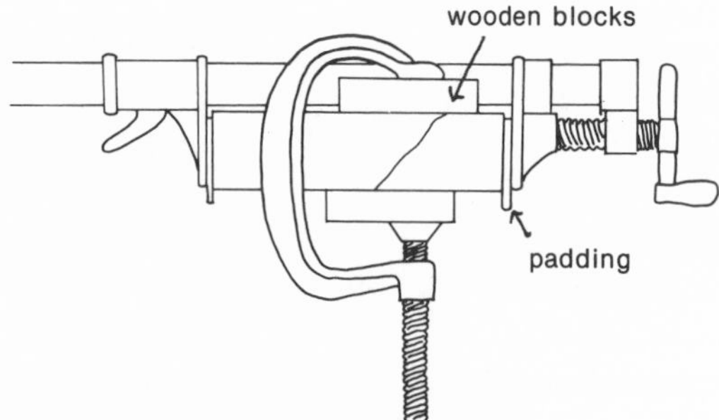

Fig. 4.2: Clamping a diagonal split.

If the piece is cracked almost all the way through and it would take very little to split it all the way, then do so. Split pieces are easier to spread with glue. If it won't split *easily* then wedge the crack open as much as you safely can. Push the nozzle of the glue bottle into the crack and squeeze hard to force the glue into the crack. Take a piece of stiff paper (the corner of an envelope, a file card) and work the glue into the crack. Clamp the piece and wipe off the excess glue. If the pieces start to slide apart along the "fault line", as in the case of a diagonal split, you may need to clamp blocks of wood on opposite sides of the part to keep it in line (Fig. 4.2). I like to let glued parts set all day or overnight before removing the clamps regardless of what the glue bottle says.

If some previous owner has used glue or wood putty unsuccessfully on the part, you have a problem. Glue will stick to wood, but it does not adhere too well to other glue. Old glue or filler should be scraped off or dug out as much as possible before you try gluing. If the old glue is yellow and looks resiny, like hardened pine sap, it might be hide glue (made from boiling animal hides) or it might be a pre-white glue commercial type such as LePage's Wood Glue. Either of these should chip out rather easily. If it is a translucent white color, it's probably a white glue (Elmer's). This will not chip or dig out without taking some of the wood with it. But don't despair; white glue is water soluble and can be soaked loose. Just be careful not to soak the wood too much or you may ruin the finish or cause the wood to swell up and split somewhere else.

Let me take a moment here to say a few words about glues. White glue or yellow wood glues are the best for gluing wood. If a piece has been properly clamped while drying, the wood will split before the glue will ever let go. Household cement (Testor's, Duco) tends to soak into wood; save it for broken dishes. These new super adhesives (Wonder Bond, Super Glue) hold very well, just like the commercials say. But they're rather unstable; a sharp side blow can cause them to part. They can be hazardous to use; also they grab too quickly and don't give you enough time to align the parts. Forget hot glue guns; the glue is too thick and it doesn't always hold well on wood. Epoxy cement is excellent, but it has to be mixed and it's hard to clean up. However, epoxy will hold on metal, and white glue won't. So save the epoxy for wood-on-metal joints, broken flyers, or any other joint that can't be clamped while it dries and use white glue for everything else. More on gluing flyers later.

Wheel rims. Loose wheel rims can be easily glued like splits and cracks, but they require a slightly different method of clamping. With a bench vise or an assistant holding the wheel, wrap some sturdy cotton (*not* plastic) clothesline twice around the wheel loosely and tie a square knot (Fig. 4.3). Slip a sturdy stick about one foot long under one round of rope and twist like a tourniquet (Fig. 4.4). Proceed cautiously—on an old wheel there's danger of damaging the rim and collapsing the wheel. Gently tapping with a hammer or mallet may encourage the wheel sections to draw together better. To keep the clamp from loosening while the glue dries, tie the tightening stick down to the wheel rim. Better yet, go buy yourself a band clamp. This is a length of nylon webbing with a tightening device on it. It's handy for a lot of things.

With a wheel rim, *always* dry clamp before you glue! Rim pegs or loose spokes may keep the rim from drawing in tight. Sometimes you may have to remove the rim pegs to get the rim to draw up properly, and replace them later. To hold a rim flat while you tighten loose joints, here's another trick that might help. Get two boards at least an inch thick and clamp them on opposite sides of the affected joint (Fig. 4.5). This works on the same principal as a tennis racket clamp to hold the rim flat while the glue dries.

A good example of re-gluing a wheel rim is my German-American Saxony wheel, which I have named Gollywampus. Over a period of time, wood can shrink across the grain, causing a round wheel with the wood grain all running the same way (as mine does) to become oval. And if the spoke and hub unit is good and solid (like mine), instead of becoming oval the rim will start to gap at the joints (which it did). One solution is to fill the gaps with pieces of wood. I took the alternate method. First I numbered all the parts with pencil to be sure that I got it back together

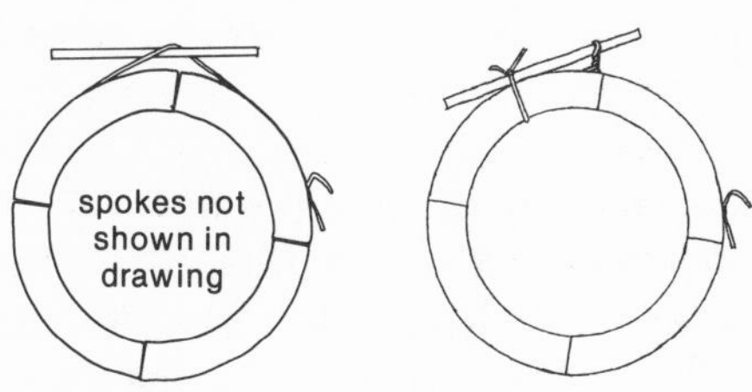

Fig. 4.3 & 4.4: Tourniquet clamp

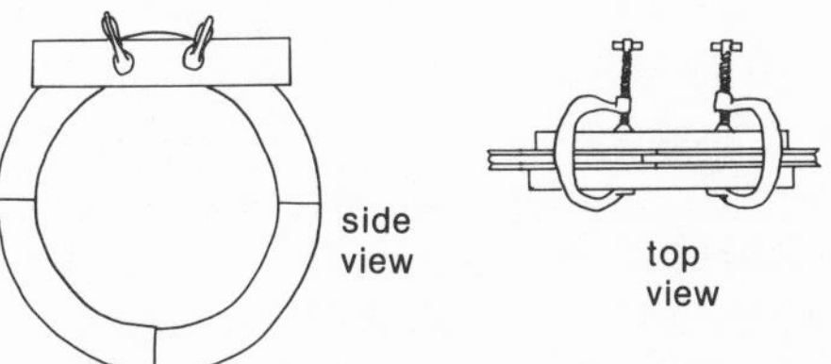

Glue joint, sandwich between 1" or 2" x 4" or larger and clamp *tightly*. Often used in conjunction with a tourniquet clamp.

Fig. 4.5: Clamping to flatten a warped joint.

properly. Then I took the rim apart, which wasn't very hard because it was halfway apart already. I cleaned off the old glue and removed broken pegs. Then I reassembled the rim using new pegs to align it, a band clamp to hold it together tight, and lots of white glue to keep it that way. I also clamped it between boards to (hopefully) flatten the rim. Next I sanded down opposite sides of the spoke unit until I could fit it back into the rim. Finally I pegged the spoke unit to the wheel rim. The wheel is now slightly oval and not *absolutely* flat, so it humps one way and wobbles the other. But it's solid and it spins well, so I just chalk it up to "character".

Loose legs and posts. We have two things that our forefathers didn't; easy-to-use glue and central heating. Now you are probably thinking, "The glue part I understand, but what's central heating got to do with spinning wheels?" Simply this; unless you have a humidifier or live in a warm climate, the air in your house will be much drier in the winter than in the summer. And this will cause your spinning wheel to dry out and the wood to shrink. Sometimes it will cause parts to loosen and legs to fall out. Furthermore, many older spinning wheels were not glued together at all—careful fitting, pegs and wedges held them together.

The oldtime woodworkers knew what they were doing and many of our modern "improvements" are more of a hinderance than a help. Most posts and legs were a tapered fit in a tapered hole. Thus, when a piece shrank and loosened it could just be tapped in with a mallet and would continue to fit tightly. Sometimes this is all that an old spinning wheel needs. One word of caution; tap gently and use a rawhide or rubber mallet so that you don't mar the wood. If all you have is a hammer, you can use this *if* you place a small block of wood between the hammer and the piece you are hitting to protect it.

Sometimes, though, a spinning wheel needs more than just a few whacks with a mallet. Modern wheels often have straight fit holes. If the part shrinks there are only two things that you can do. You can glue it. Or if the part must be able to move or come out, you can shim it; that is, you can wrap it with paper to take up the slack. Be sure to use a firm paper such as grocery bag or brown wrapping paper. Cut an ample strip and wrap it around the post. This is known as a shim. How many times you wrap the paper around depends on how loose the fit is. One to three times is usually plenty.

If you need more than six wraps, you don't need paper, you need leather. Sometimes parts from several spinning wheels are used to make one complete wheel (known as a composite), or sometimes parts will be badly worn. If there is a good deal of space to fill, line the hole with thin leather. Use something about the thickness of suede. Scraps from sewing or crafts, elbow patches, old purses or clothes, anything is useable. Do *not* use plastic, cloth, cardboard, toothpicks or tape. Don't laugh! I've seen spinning wheels where people have used any and all of the above. And *you've* never had to peel petrified adhesive tape off of wood! Please! For minor problems wrap the post with paper. To cure a sloppier fit, line the hole with a single thickness of leather with a tiny bit of glue in the hole to hold it in place. Put the parts back together and trim off the excess paper or leather with a sharp knife.

The distaff holder, at least on old wheels,

is always a tapered fit in a tapered hole. This was so that the distaff could be swung around to a comfortable working position and yet it would stay put. And strangely enough, the taper is usually identical to the spigot reamer that my great-grandfather bought for making spigot holes in wine barrels. That spigot reamer has come in very handy for reshaping worn distaff holes. If your distaff hole is worn and you don't have a spigot reamer, try a leather shim.

Now of course there are exceptions to shimming, usually where the wheel spokes fit into the hub. If you can get the loose spoke out, beautiful! But if you can't (usually because of the rim) try (with caution) the solution that my dad came up with. I will quote directly from his two-cents-worth. "Drill a 1/8" (diameter) hole diagonally through the base of the spoke (Fig. 4.6) and pump it full of glue [author's note: stick the nozzle of the glue bottle into the hole and squeeze *hard*] and drive a 1/8" dowel rod into the hole. Hydraulic action forces the glue well into the joint and when it dries you have a solid spoke again. Please don't use nails." When the glue is dry, cut the dowel off flush with the spoke and/or hub and stain it to match. This is very useful on wool wheels where the spoke has shrunk and become a sloppy fit in the hub, but where there might be a nail through the rim which prevents you from taking the spoke out to glue it. The same goes for spinning assembly wheels, but only if the spoke has become a *very* sloppy fit. If the spoke has simply become unglued (you can twist it but you can't wiggle it) securely pegging it to the rim is often sufficient.

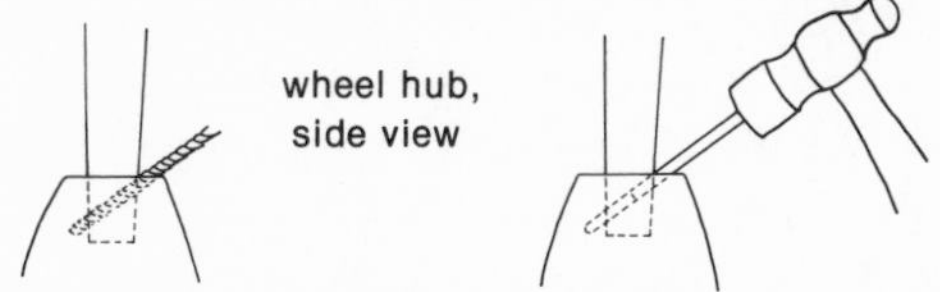

Fig. 4.6 & 4.7: Pegging a shrunken spoke that cannot be removed.

Aligning the wheel. Tap the wheel posts in tight and then check the alignment of the wheel. If the wheel runs steady but leans a little vertically, check the axle slots. A sloppy fitting axle slot means bad design, poor craftsmanship or improper assembly. If one of the axle slots is deeper than the other causing the wheel to run at an angle, or worse yet rub on the post, line the bottom of the slot with thin, soft lead, brass or copper, or a piece of leather (Fig. 4.8). If the slot is too wide and the axle slops around sideways as well, make the leather strip wide enough to cover the bottom of the slot and extend up the sides cradling the axle (Fig. 4.9).

If they are not badly worn or uneven, then the problem is in the posts. Remove the post on the lower side of the axle by driving out the peg and then tapping the post on the bottom with a mallet to loosen it. Shim it with paper as described above. This will raise it up out of the bench. If the wheel is okay vertically but does not line

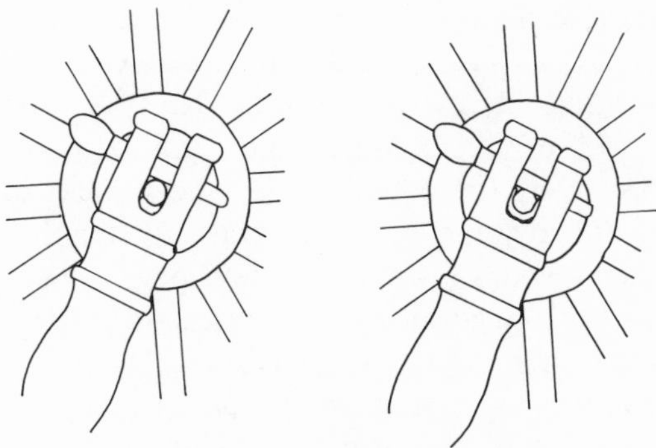

Fig. 4.8 & 4.9: Leveling axle slots

up with the spinning assembly, put a small strip of thin leather behind one side of the axle to bring the wheel into line. If the axle slot fits well, then one of the posts is leaning too far back. You can scrape down and fit the "high" wheel post until the axle will ride level, or you can shim up the low wheel post. Tap it loose and place a couple of layers of paper or a strip of thin leather in the hole under the low side of the post. This should bring the post to a more upright position and bring the wheel into proper alignment.

Missing pegs. Another simple problem to solve is missing pegs. Since most older spinning wheels were held together exclusively with pegs and wedges, you will no doubt have a few to replace. Broken pegs must be removed before you can make a replacement. Please note: some pegs were a tapered fit, particularly wheel axle pegs and the pegs or wedges holding the wheel posts in. To remove these, first find the small end of the peg. Then find a piece of dowel rod or metal rod the same diameter or slightly smaller. Take a hammer or mallet and use the rod to drive the broken peg out of the hole from the small end.

Most spinning wheels were built with portability and ease of repair in mind. The pegs could be driven out and the whole spinning wheel would come apart for easy packing in a trunk bound for the new world or a covered wagon going West. However, the actual drive wheel was not meant to come apart and was put together with what is known as "blind pegs"—pegs that do not go all the way through. If these are broken (you can tell by wiggling the spoke) they will have to be drilled out. Take a drill, either hand or electric, and a drill bit in a standard dowel rod size as close to the original peg size as possible. Study the angle of the original hole and try to follow it as close as you can. An assistant to hold the wheel steady is helpful. Be careful not to drill all the way through. Next, take a piece of dowel rod the same diameter as the hole that you drilled and drive it in. A drop of glue in the hole first doesn't hurt. Cut the dowel off flush with the hole and stain the end of it to match the spinning wheel.

To replace pegs that go all the way through, you will need a piece of dowel rod the size of the larger end of the peg. If the peg is not an exact dowel rod size, use the next size larger. Whittle or file it down until you have a proper fit. Drive it in good and tight, *without* glue, and cut the ends off flush with the piece it's driven through. Stain to match.

There are some exceptions to the above. The wheel axle pegs have to be easily removable so that you can take the wheel in and out (Fig. 4.10). In this case, let the peg stick out about ¼" (6mm) on the small end

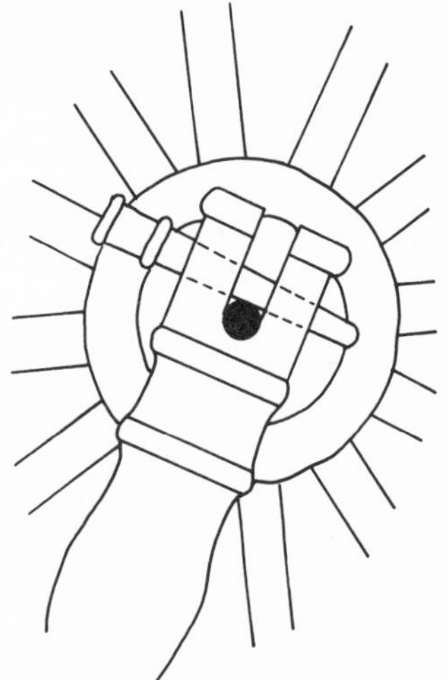

Fig. 4.10: Removable wheel axle peg

and give yourself about ¾" (2cm) on the large to grasp. If you want something fancier or you have one of the original pegs, go to a woodworker and have him turn you up a peg with a proper knob on the end. Be sure to bring the wheel posts so that he can fit the peg to the hole, and of course, bring the peg that you want copied. If you don't have an original peg, bring one of the maidens so that the finial can be copied for the peg knob.

On a spinning wheel with a bobbin-lead or flyer-lead spinning assembly the brake band usually has one end fastened to a tapered wooden peg. This peg has a knob, often flattened, and is used to tighten or loosen the brake band, much the same as you would tune the strings on a violin. This must always stay tightly where it's put, so if you are replacing it be sure that the taper of the peg matches the taper of the hole exactly.

If the wheel posts are crosspegged under the bench to hold them in, you will find either round pegs or a cross between a peg and a wedge. A hole or slot was drilled in the post and a tapered peg or a rounded off wedge was driven in. As it was driven, it forced the wheel post down into the hole more tightly. On older spinning wheels you will often find that the wheel posts have settled farther into the hole than was intended. Especially wool wheels. This means that often there is a gap between the hole or slot and the bench. So simply repegging it won't do any good. You can deepen the hole or slot, shim the post, or use an idea that my dad came up with, which I called a stepped wedge (Fig. 4.11). This is a wedge with a notch cut in it to accommodate the difference between the hole and the bench.

Wedges are also found where a piece, such as a leg, comes all the way through another, such as the bench. The end of the leg was split with a saw and a wedge the same width of the cut but slightly thicker was made. The parts were assembled and the wedge was driven in and cut off flush. Wedges seldom came out and became lost, but you may need to replace the existing wedges with thicker ones.

Sometimes a leg was "blind wedged". This means that a blind hole (one that does not go all the way through) was drilled in the bench, the leg was split, and a wedge the proper length, width and thickness was made. The wedge was started into the cut and then the leg was driven into the hole. As the leg was driven in, the wedge was forced into the leg by the end of the hole. This was a one-shot deal; you did it right the first time! It also demanded good judgement. The wedge had to be thick enough to hold the leg securely, but it couldn't be too thick or too long or the leg wouldn't go all the way in.

Many modern wheel builders think that with today's modern glues and precision machinery and measuring tools they don't need to cross peg joints. Not so. My first spinning wheel was built from scratch by

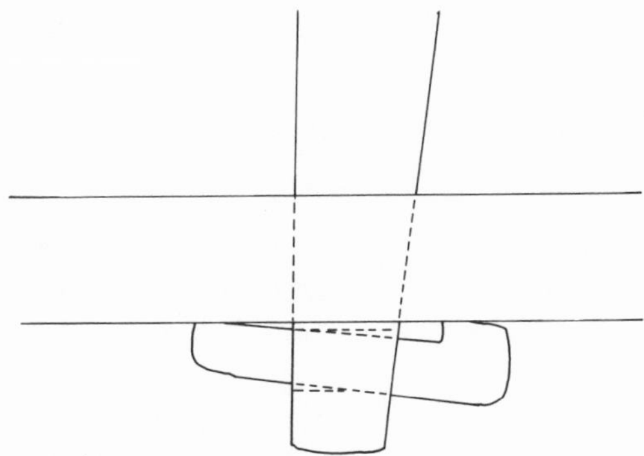

Fig. 4.11: Stepped wedge

my dad, a tool and die maker used to working in thousandths of an inch. All the joints were a beautifully tight fit, no glue needed. It stayed tight for a little over a year. Two winters in a centrally-heated home and we had to go back and cross peg most of the joints. The main upright posts were still tight because they had been wedged to begin with.

If your spinning wheel develops a lot of very loose joints over the winter (a *little* looseness is normal) make sure that you didn't have it setting too near a heat register or radiator. Tap the parts back in with a mallet and glue or shim if necessary. And I strongly recommend cross pegging the following: the rear maiden, the mother-of-all and the support post, and the two parts of the distaff holder where they meet. After all, it's not easy to spin flax when your distaff keeps flopping over sideways! On an upright wheel, I would also peg the upright posts and their cross braces where they meet. Be especially careful to peg securely any parts that you may use to carry the spinning wheel by.

It's a very simple matter to peg a joint. Drill a dowel rod sized hole; 3/16" (4.8mm) is good. Drive in a piece of dowel and cut it off flush with both sides. Be sure that the dowel is a good fit. On many of the older spinning wheels the builders assured a good fit by driving a square peg into a round hole. This squared the hole slightly and rounded the peg, wedging it in securely.

Missing parts. Next to missing pegs, your biggest problem with an antique will probably be missing parts. This gets a little more complicated. If the piece is one of the legs, maidens, wheel posts or spokes, take the remaining leg, etc., to a woodworker and have him turn you up a duplicate. Be sure to match the wood grain as well as the style. If it is a piece that is not one of a set, such as the high leg on a Saxony or wool wheel or part of the distaff holder, study the style of the rest of the spinning wheel. The high leg is usually a longer version of the shorter legs, and the distaff holder pieces can often be slightly thinner copies of the wheel posts. Likewise if you have to make both of the maidens.

If you have to make the entire distaff holder, be aware that the measurements vary from spinning wheel to spinning wheel. When in use, the distaff should sit an inch or two (2.5cm to 5cm) in front of the orifice and a couple of inches above it. Explain this to the woodworker and let him measure what will be needed.

As far as the distaff itself is concerned, study pictures and diagrams in books. A simple "birdcage" distaff can be made using rattan balloon sticks or thin dowel rod for the ribs. A sturdier birdcage distaff can be built by making a bending jig (Fig. 4.12) to bend 1/4" (7mm) dowel rod that has been softened by boiling it for several hours or soaking it for a day. Simpler yet, buy an

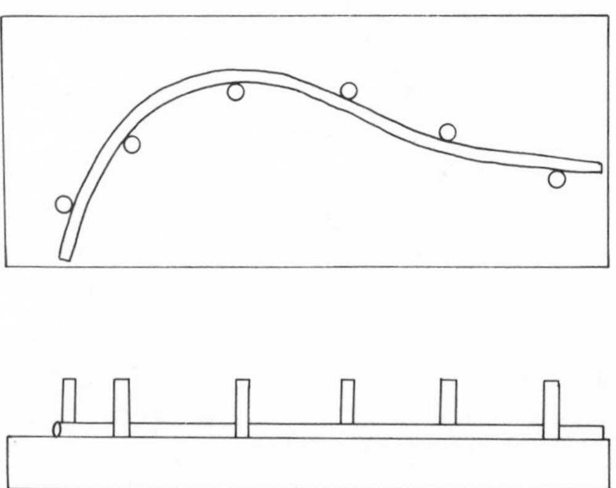

Fig. 4.12: Bending jig for distaff ribs

unfinished distaff from a spinning supplier. But if you insist on building your own, a lantern distaff (Fig. 4.13) is probably the simplest. If your spinning wheel is European, a pole type distaff might be more authentic. But if you're more concerned with function than appearance, I would recommend a good sturdy birdcage type.

A much simpler part to replace is the footman. That's the connecting rod between the wheel and the treadle. In an emergency you can use a piece of heavy string or cord. Double it over and knot the doubled end to form a loop. Slip the loop over the crank and tie the other end to the treadle. One word of caution though. Do not take your foot off the treadle and let it coast; the cord tends to wind around the crank until something breaks, and it might not be the cord!

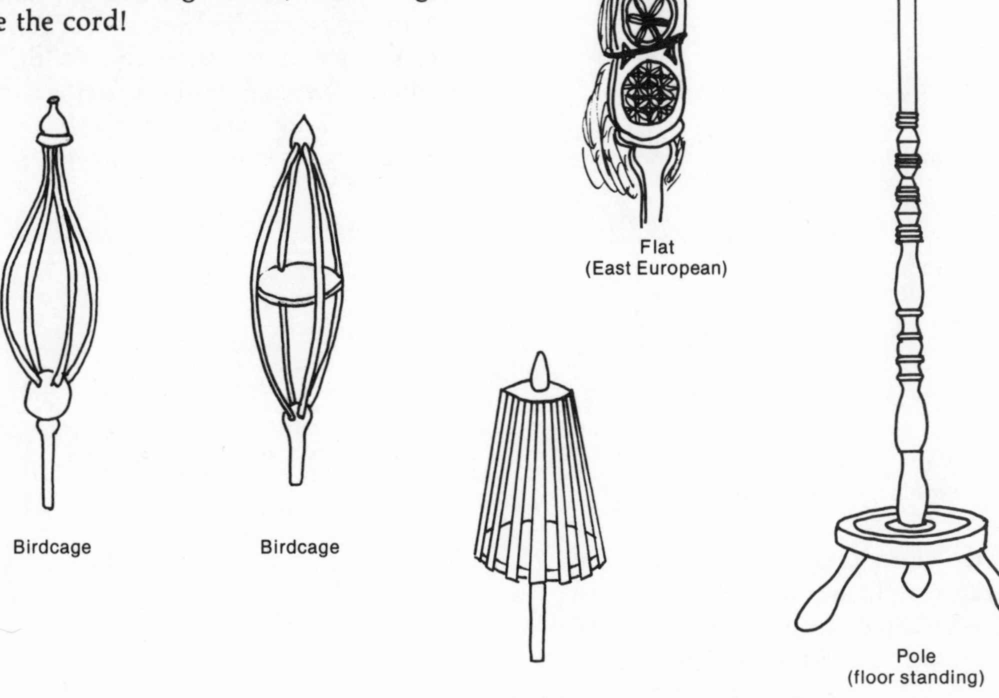

Fig. 4.13

For a much more permanent and authentic footman, take a strip of hardwood about 1" to 1½" (3cm or 4cm) wide and ¼" (7mm) thick and cut a keyhole in one end (Fig. 4.14). Next, prop the end of the backbar of the treadle about 1" off the floor and measure from the crank in its lowest position to the top of the treadle. On the footman measure down from the top of the keyhole to the same measurement and cut the footman off to this length. Drill one or two ¹/₈" (2mm) holes in the bottom end of the footman, round the edges and ends if you like and sand it smooth. Stain and/or varnish it to match your spinning wheel and use a leather thong to fasten it to the treadle.

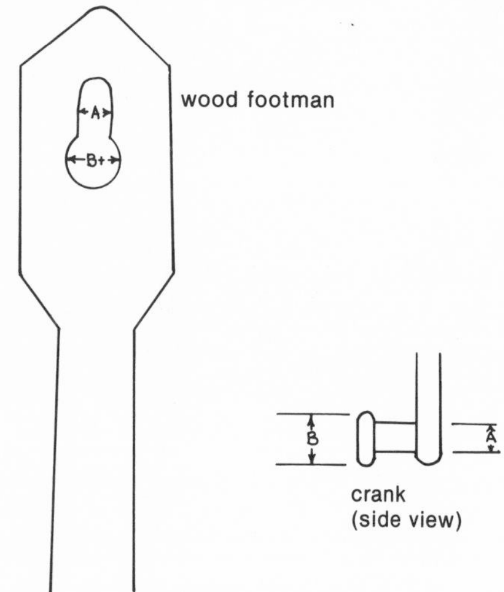

Fig. 4.14: Keyhole for a wood footman

When the crank is in its lowest position, the treadle should be parallel to or at a slight upward angle from the floor. Typically, it should be ½" to 1" (2cm to 3cm) off the floor. Be sure that the footman is short enough. A treadle that thumps is both annoying and ineffective.

If you have a spinning wheel with a heel-and-toe type treadle (see chapter 10) a cord footman will not work, as you are pushing with the footman as well as pulling on it. You must have a rigid footman. Wood is the easiest material to work with, and the most authentic on an antique. On some modern spinning wheels you can use a metal bar, or metal rod with loops bent in both ends. Either way it should not have a "keyhole". It should have a single round hole the size of the end of the crank. The crank will have a screw knob of some sort to hold the footman on. This way, when you press with your heel on the treadle and cause the treadle to push upward on the footman, it will not jump off the crank as a "keyhole" would.

Something else that you will probably have to replace is the leather bearings that hold the spinning assembly. With rare exceptions they will be a flat leather on the front and a loop leather on the back (Fig. 4.15). The front maiden will have a slot in

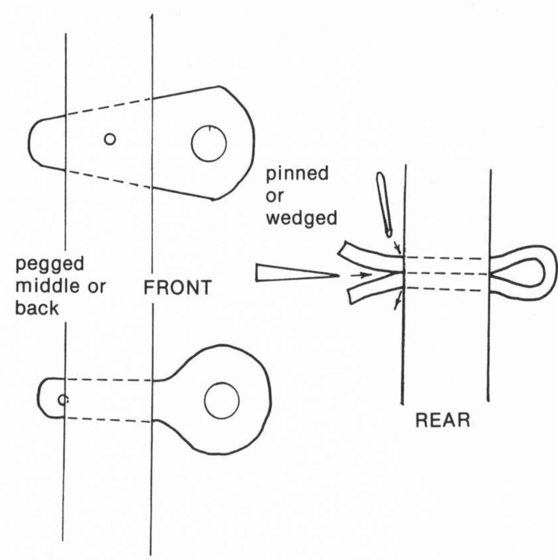

Fig. 4.15: Leather bearings

it that is tapered from about 1" x 3/16" (25mm x 6mm) to about 1/2" x 3/16" (12mm x 6mm). A very thick, stiff piece of leather, sometimes several layers pegged together, is inserted in this slot with a rounded end about 1" (2.5cm) across sticking out with a hole in it to hold the spinning assembly. The back maiden, or on some uprights the tension adjustment, will have a round or square straight hole ranging in size from ¼" (7mm) to ½" (13mm) square. A strip of slightly thinner leather was folded over to form a loop and the ends were pushed through the hole and wedged or pegged on the other side. These leathers became rather petrified with age and grease, and sometimes they've worn out, cracked or broken off completely. On some new spinning wheels the "leathers" may be inadequate and you may wish to replace them. They are not difficult to replace, but you need the right materials. For the front leather, if at all possible go to your friendly neighborhood shoe repair shop and ask for a scrap of "sole leather". This will be almost ¼" (7mm) thick and the scraps that he throws out should be big enough for your needs. If you can't get sole leather, get some 9-10 oz. or 10-11 oz. "tooling cowhide" from a craft shop or laminate several layers of thinner cowhide together with white glue and clamp them between blocks of wood to dry.

To make a pattern, take a piece of cardboard and fit and trim and fit and trim until it fits the slot exactly. Mark where the edge of the maiden comes and extend the wider end to form a circle at least 1" (2.5cm) in diameter. If the slot extends all the way through the maiden, and most of them do, it's a good idea to allow a ¼" (7mm) tail to stick out the small side of the slot. When you have a pattern that seems to fit, trace it onto the piece of leather and cut it out using a jig saw or coping saw, a mallet and chisel, or failing that, a *sharp* knife. When you have it cut out, check the fit. You might have to trim or file the edges to get it to fit properly. Next, take a drill bit 1/64" larger than the head of the spinning assembly (see diagram) and drill a hole in the center of the large end of the leather. The spindle head should be a loose fit in this hole, but should not slop around. Also, it should not fall through the hole; the leather should rest up against the shoulder of the spindle head. To antique the leather and also to harden it, I color it with dark brown leather dye. When you're satisfied with the color and fit of the leather, put it in place and crosspeg it either through the maiden or through the tail of the leather.

To replace the rear leather bearing, take a strip of 4-5 oz. or 6-7 oz. tooling leather (craft cowhide) about 1/8" (3mm) thick and cut it to the width of the hole, slightly wider where the loop will be (see diagram). This type of leather can be cut with a pair of heavy duty scissors or a small pair of tinsnips or with a sharp knife. The strip of leather should be long enough to form a loop the size of the tail of the spindle and still leave a ½" (12mm) tail sticking out the other side of the maiden. Color the leather if desired (clamp it bent into its final position to dry) and fit it in place. Drive a small wedge in between the tails on the other side to hold it. The tail of the spinning assembly is slid into the rear (loop) leather and the front maiden is twisted to slide the front (flat) leather onto the head of the spinning assembly. Incidentally, the above described loop-type leather is also used on the wool wheel head to hold the spindle. But in this case, they were made of either leather or braided cornhusk.

And now to the important part of the spinning wheel, the spinning assembly. The problems that you are most likely to have with this unit (besides missing parts) are a broken flyer, worn out or missing hooks and chipped, split or worn out bobbin ends and pulleys on an antique spinning wheel, and a binding bobbin; or, on a modern wheel, an insufficient difference in size between the pulleys.

A broken flyer is no problem *providing* you have both pieces and it is a clean fresh break, that is, no one else has tried gluing it. If your luck is holding and the break is repairable, you will need some five-minute epoxy cement, a watch or clock, and a comfortable chair. A chair in front of the TV is nice. Assemble everything that you will need and then mix up the epoxy as per the directions on the tube. Spread the epoxy on the break and join the pieces. Be sure they're lined up correctly. Excess epoxy can be trimmed off after it has hardened. It's hard to clamp an oddly shaped piece like a flyer, so you just have to sit there and hold it together with your hands for the next 10, or better yet 15, minutes. Then you can *carefully* set it down. But be sure to let the epoxy cure completely before you try doing any further work on the part. Wait a couple of hours at least.

If you do not have a clean surface to glue, that is, it was previously glued and has come apart, scrape, dig or soak as much of the old glue out as you can and try the five-minute epoxy as described above. I don't guarantee anything, but I've had pretty good luck with it.

If the epoxy won't hold or if you are missing one of the broken parts, you will have to take or send the entire spinning assembly and what you have of the flyer to a spinning wheel restorer and have a new flyer made. If you're good at woodworking you *can* make the flyer yourself, but it's rather tricky to get it lined up and fitted properly. First you will need to make a paper pattern using the remainder of the broken flyer. You will also need a piece of wood ¾″ (2cm) thick. Stay away from pine (too soft) and oak (too hard and open grained). Maple or birch are good. Trace the pattern onto the wood, making sure that the grain runs the length of the flyer. When you make your pattern, draw half of it, fold the paper in half, and cut it out. Line the ends of the arms of the flyer up with a straightedge of the wood and trace. Then fold the pattern in half the way you cut it out and lay it back on your tracing and draw the center (fold) line. This will make it easier to drill the hole straight and centered if you are using a drill press. Carefully cut the flyer out using a jig saw or coping saw.

Next, drill the hole for the metal shaft. On an antique spinning wheel this part of the shaft is likely to be square; on a modern spinning wheel it will probably be round. Either way make the hole the same size diameter as this portion of the shaft. Now the hole must be perfectly centered and straight, and the shaft must line up equidistant with both arms of the flyer or it will not run smoothly. If at all possible, use a drill press, even if you have to borrow your neighbor's. Stand the flyer up on the table of the drill press, using a carpenter's square or a right angle plate to assure that it stands straight and square. Use the center line you drew to center the hole. If all you have is a hand-held electric drill, I wish you luck. Clamp the flyer in a bench vice so that you will have both hands free to hold the drill and get an assistant to help you sight it. Cross your fingers that it comes out straight and true. To fit the flyer to a square shaft, take a narrow square file and work at the hole until you have a perfect fit. The flyer should fit tightly up against the head of the shaft. There should be enough room inside of the flyer for the bobbin to spin freely with the flyer pulley tightly in place. The bobbin should not rub against the flyer, and the flyer must not extend beyond the bobbin pulley or it will catch on the drive band. Also be sure to round the edges of the flyer and sand it smooth, especially where the thread will be rubbing on it.

Missing hooks are a little easier to replace. A hook will either wear through and break off or the wood will split and the hook will fall out. A split flyer should be glued and clamped before you do anything else. Broken off hooks should be pulled out with a pliers. If the hook has broken off flush with the wood and you can't get the &=!† thing out, you will have to carefully drill a new hole as close as possible to the old hook. If the other hooks are "L" shaped or if you want to be very authentic, find some steel wire the same guage as the rest of the hooks. Rusty looks the most authentic. Shape the hook and then set it into a pre-drilled hole. If the hooks are a more rounded shape, or if you are replacing the entire set of hooks, buy the smallest size screw eyes available and open them up with a pliers to form hooks. Then simply screw them into place. On a replacement flyer be sure to drill holes first so that you don't split the wood getting the hooks in. One other point; if you are making a new flyer, the end hooks should line up just inside the ends of the bobbin. How many hooks you use will depend on how big the spinning assembly is and what size yarn you will be spinning. On an average sized antique replacement used for spinning traditionally thin yarn, I have used as many as eight hooks to a side. A smaller spinning assembly or one for thick yarn can have as few as five. But for thick yarn be sure to use larger hooks. On modern spinning wheels I find that brass cup hooks work nicely.

If the entire bobbin is missing, either go to a spinning wheel restorer or read the next chapter. Chipped bobbin ends are simpler to replace. If the chips are small, don't worry about them. But if they're big enough to catch the yarn or cause the drive band to jump off, then that end should be replaced. The missing area can be filled in with wood putty, but I feel that this should be used *only* as a temporary measure, as it looks very makeshift and cheap and doesn't always work too well. A competent woodworker should be able to make a new bobbin end using the broken pieces as a pattern. Many bobbin ends were just a force fit, so you should have no problem getting it off. Break it off if you have to. The new end should be glued in place and stained to match. Be sure that the new end is perfectly centered and exactly the same size as the old one.

I have noticed that on many of the older spinning wheels, the bobbin ends are end grain. This means that the wood grain runs the thickness of the bobbin end, not the diameter. As these age and split, they form cracks that no amount of gluing and clamping will bring together. If this has loosened the fit of the end, and it usually has, then you will have to replace the end. If the bobbin end still fits tight, you can fill the crack with wood putty but I would recommend replacing the end. If the crack is small and doesn't catch the thread, just learn to live with it and leave well enough alone.

The purpose of the tension adjustment in relation to the double pulley spinning assembly is to allow a certain amount of slippage on the bobbin pulley so that the spinner can hold the yarn back until it accumulates sufficient twist to hold together. Over years of use this will wear the groove in the bobbin pulley very deep. There comes a point where the spinning wheel does not work efficiently any more. I have seen attempts to build up worn pulley grooves using everything from linen thread to wood putty to rubber bands. None of these work very well, especially the rubber bands. You are much better off having the pulley replaced.

If the bobbin is intact but won't turn freely or maybe doesn't turn at all, it probably needs cleaning. Remove the bobbin, clean the shaft with coarse steel wool, and scrape out the hole down the center of the bobbin. If you put it back together and it still won't spin freely, or you have a new spinning wheel with a stubborn bobbin, either the hole is too small or the bobbin is being pushed against the flyer by the flyer pulley. A round file can be used to enlarge the bobbin hole. If the flyer pulley goes on too far, fill in a row or two of the threads on the spindle with solder.

Of course before you can do anything to the bobbin you have to remove it from the spinning assembly. With a bobbin-lead or flyer-lead spinning assembly this is no problem. You can just slide the bobbin off the end. With a double-pulley spinning assembly, however, you must first remove the flyer pulley. The flyer pulleys on some antiques may be rusted solid. Others were probably never removed from the day the spinning wheel was built and have become glued solid by dirt and grease. If the pulley does not come off easily, DO NOT USE FORCE! Use oil. I stand the spinning assembly up on end and apply a couple of drops of penetrating oil to the pulley nut. Let it set over night. If it doesn't come off fairly easily, try the oil a second time. I have yet to meet a pulley that did not respond to this treatment.

When you are trying to remove the pulley, *do not* grasp the flyer as something to twist against. The flyer is the most delicate part of the spinning wheel and you run the risk of breaking it. Instead, either stick a screwdriver or other tool through the exit holes on the spindle head, or hold the spindle head with a pliers. Then twist.

And be sure that you are twisting the pulley in the right direction. Antique spinning wheels usually used a left-handed thread. Some newer spinning wheels use a conventional right-handed thread.

On a new spinning wheel, loose bobbin ends can simply be glued, as can a loose flyer. Use white glue for the bobbin, epoxy cement for the flyer. Not enough hooks? Find some matching screw-in hooks at the hardware store and add a few. The most serious problem is an insufficient difference in size between the bobbin and flyer pulleys, causing too weak a feed-on. The best solution for this is to take the bobbin(s) to a woodworker and have him deepen the pulley grooves. If the bobbin pulleys are rather small already, have a larger flyer pulley made.

If you do need a new flyer pulley (old or new) take the entire spinning assembly to a good woodworker, or better yet a spinning wheel restorer. He will need the old pulley for size and style and for the metal nut or set screw that holds it on the spindle. If the old pulley (and the metal nut) is missing, don't bother with a woodworker, find a spinning wheel restorer.

If the metal spindle shaft is broken or worn out, take it to a restorer. Or read Chapter 7, "Do It Yourself". If the spindle is missing you'll just have to go to a restorer, because chances are that the rest of the spinning assembly is missing too.

The wool wheel spindle is much easier to replace. Take a piece of 3/16" (4.5mm) diameter steel rod, cut it to length (the distance between the leathers, plus 8" [21cm]) and round one end. Point the other end like a knitting needle. Have a woodworker turn a wooden pulley (see Figs 1.6, 1.7 and 1.8) and epoxy it in place.

Moving now to the bottom of the spinning wheel, let's talk about the treadle. The condition of the treadle is a good indication of how much use the spinning wheel has had. Some of these will be quite worn, but they are rarely completely worn out. Sometimes broken and occasionally missing, but rarely worn out. If the treadle on your spinning wheel does have broken or missing pieces, they can easily be replaced by a good woodworker. Use the original pieces or the marks left by them as a pattern. Be sure to match the wood; most early American spinning wheels had treadles of oak, but European wheel makers used whatever grew in their region.

If the entire treadle is missing, a new one can be made without too much difficulty (Fig. 4.16). Measure the distance between the two front legs at the pivot holes and make the pivot bar* this long. It should be about 1½" (4cm) thick, either square or rounded. Lay it in place and measure from a point a couple of inches in from the left end, to a point directly under the wheel crank. This will be the size and location of the back bar,* which is usually about 1" (2.5cm) wide and ½" (12mm) thick. The front end of the back bar fits into a notch in the pivot bar and is pegged and sometimes glued in place. The far end has one or two small holes to tie the footman to the treadle. A flat board about ¼" (6mm) thick and about 3" to 4" (8cm to 10cm) wide in the front tapering to about 2" (5cm) wide in the back connects the pivot bar and the back bar. This footboard* also rests in a notch in the pivot bar and is pegged (see diagram). For the metal pivot pins in the ends of the pivot bar I recommend using 20 penny common nails with the heads sawed off.

*Having found no proper names for the parts of the treadle, I have given them my own self-descriptive names for the purposes of this book.

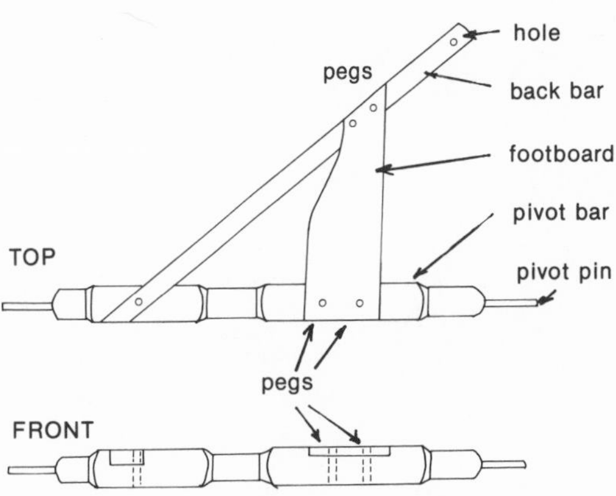

Fig. 4.16: Pivot Treadle (Early American and Saxony Wheel)

If your spinning wheel has a hinged treadle (Fig. 4.17), it will not have pivot holes in the front legs. This type of treadle is much the same as a pivoting treadle, except that the front bar is separate from the back bar and footboard. Also, the front bar is usually about 2" (5cm) wide by ¾" (2cm) thick with holes in the ends for the front legs to fit through. The two parts are hinged together using sturdy but flexible leather. Four-five oz. cowhide is good for the hinges. Use the notches and markings on the treadle pieces to tell you what size to make the hinge pieces. Large carpet tacks are good for fastening them in place.

For those of you interested in complete restoration, I will say a few words about ivory half-spokes, knobs and finials. These are sometimes found on exceptionally ornate spinning wheels which were sometimes built as wedding gifts or bridal send-offs, and called bride's wheels or dowry wheels. Very often some of these ivories will be missing. They in no way effect the operation or performance of the spinning wheel, but they do contribute to its appearance. If you are very good at woodturning they are not *too* difficult to replace.

First off, they were not ivory but bone. So you get a nice thick soup bone and boil it clean and bake it dry, or you go down to the local pet shop and buy the thickest, least hollow dog bone you can find. Saw it into strips lengthwise and turn it on the lathe. Copy existing finials and be sure that you use a good sharp tool and have your tool rest as close as possible. This is where a lathe made for miniature work comes in

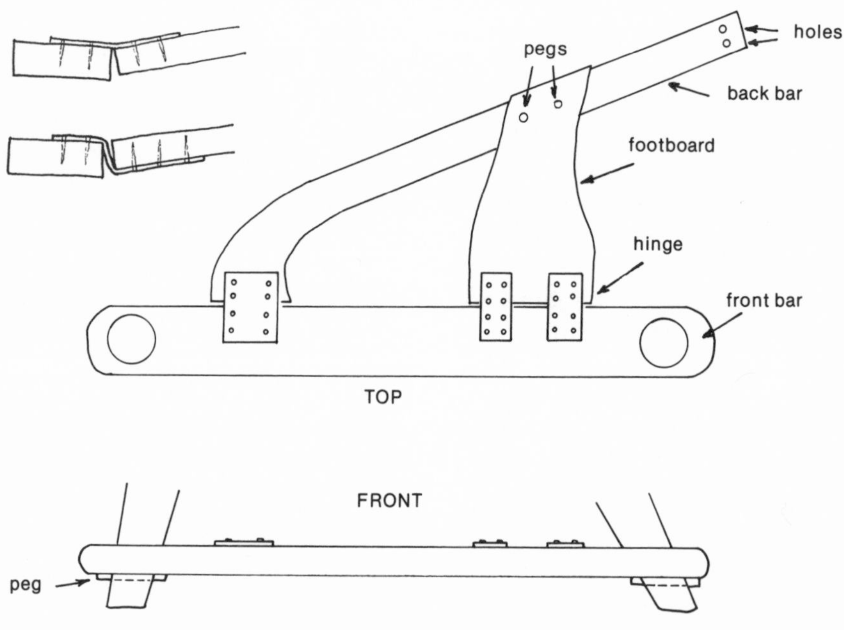

Fig. 4.17: Hinged Treadle (European Saxony)

handy, providing it has a three jaw chuck. Some tripoli buffing compound on a buffing wheel will give the piece a nice sheen and it will add some dirt and "age" in the pores of the bone. Use epoxy cement to secure it in place on the spinning wheel.

This was all discovered by trial and error when we were brought a lovely Bavarian upright that was loaded with "ivory", half of it missing. The owner wanted it *fully* restored. I took one of the finials down to a local lapidary and jewelry shop, who verified that it was indeed bone. Pet shop dog bone was the only thing available to us. Dad did the turning, I did the buffing, and we were both surprised and pleased with the results. But not as surprised or pleased as the owner of the spinning wheel!

To summarize, any missing part is best left to a spinning wheel restorer to replace, but with a little care and the proper tools and materials, there are many things that the wheel owner himself can fix.

V
PROFESSIONAL REPAIRS

There are some repairs that require special equipment or a thorough knowledge of spinning wheels and how they work. One fellow fell off the ladder while decorating the Christmas tree and landed on his wife's antique spinning wheel. He didn't even try to fix it, he just ran a newspaper want-ad for a spinning wheel repairman. Another woman had no idea where to get the spinning wheel she had just bought in New England restored. Flying back to Chicago, she got into a conversation with a fellow passenger who happened to be one of my spinning students, and who gave her my name and address. Some people, though, will try fixing anything themselves. In this chapter I will include directions for more advanced repairs, but please be advised that you are better off going to a spinning wheel repairman/restorer. For your convenience, I have listed as many of these repairers/restorers as I know of in the back of the book under "Sources". After all, you can't count on sitting next to a spinner on a plane.

If you have a variable speed lathe with a double chuck capability, you can repair crosswise breaks in legs, posts, etc. Such as one case I had where the wheel owner's children had used the bench of her upright wheel as a footstool and had broken both of the front legs off at the bench. Or the spinning wheel where someone had used the distaff holder cross-arm to replace a missing leg and had worn the end of it down beyond use. Or another spinning wheel where ten of the 12 spokes had been broken off at the hub. (I'd like to know how *that* one happened!)

I will describe one way to fix a broken leg, as this is the most common type of break. (Fig. 5.1) First clean the broken end

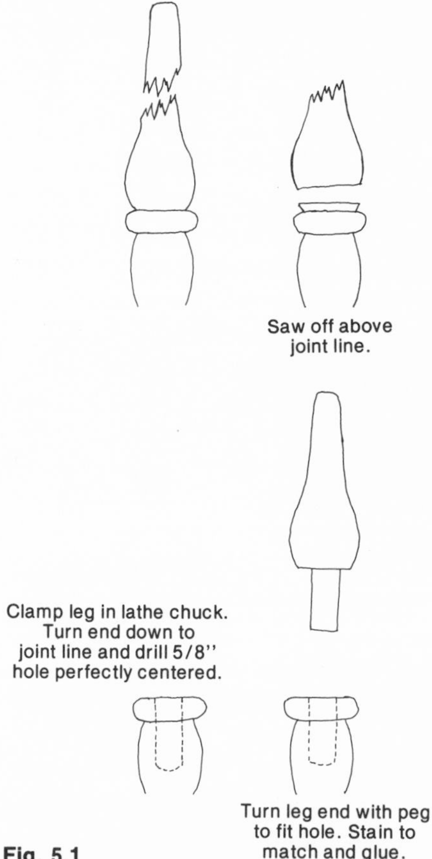

Fig. 5.1

out of the hole in the bench. Then find a line in the wood turning pattern of the leg where the joint would not show, and saw the broken end off just short of this line. Clamp the leg in the live chuck of the lathe and turn the end down to the line to get a perfectly flat, even end. Next, with the leg in one chuck, put a drill bit in the other chuck and drill a perfectly centered hole about 1" (2.5cm) to 1½" (4cm) deep in the end of the leg. For most average spinning wheel legs a 5/8" (15.5mm) drill is about right. Remove the leg and the drill bit and speed the lathe up for wood turning. Select a piece of wood that closely matches the wood grain of the leg and turn a copy of the broken-off leg end. One end should have the post that fits in the hole in the bench and the other end should have a peg that fits *snugly* into the hole that you drilled in the leg. If it turns out that you made the peg too small, cut it off and drill a 5/8" (15.5mm) hole in the piece the same as you did in the leg. Use a piece of 5/8" dowel rod to splice the leg and the end together. If the end fits tightly in the leg and the whole thing fits properly in the bench, then stain the end to match the rest of the leg and glue them together. This repair method is also used for a wheel post where a piece of the top has split off and become lost; replace the entire top end.

For broken off spokes, find a piece of dowel rod that will fit in the hole in the hub and drill a hole this size in the spoke. Use this to splice the broken off spoke back in place. BUT: Be sure that you use large enough dowel rod, that you get the holes on the spokes perfectly centered, and that you use long enough pieces of dowel. One wheel owner neglected all three of the above points on a spinning wheel where seven of the ten spokes were broken off. The result was a wheel that wobbled wildly from side to side. Fortunately we were able to get the wheel apart and re-do it. Quarter-inch dowel rod is a little small for most spokes, and a ½" long piece is not long enough to give the spoke proper stability. And most of the wobble resulted from not having the holes centered. We re-drilled the spokes, and re-doweled them with pieces 1½" long, and the wheel now runs absolutely true.

I have spoken of the necessity of perfectly centered holes, and this is not difficult to do with a double chuck lathe. But if the piece is long, narrow or slightly irregular on the end being clamped, then you run into problems. Dad solved this by making a drilling sleeve (Fig. 5.2). This can be made from a piece of large diameter dowel, and can be made to fit any job. Basically it is a piece of wood with a hole the diameter of the drill being used coming through from one end, and a slightly oversized, slightly rounded hole in the other end to accommodate the piece being drilled. This is slid onto the drill while it is stopped, and then is slipped over the piece when the drill is moved into place. The drill sleeve is hand held to help center the drill bit on the piece.

Another repair that may cause problems is threaded parts such as the tension screw. Woodthreading tap and die sets run about $40 to $60 per size, although Conover Woodcraft Specialties has come out with an assemble-your-own kit for about $30.

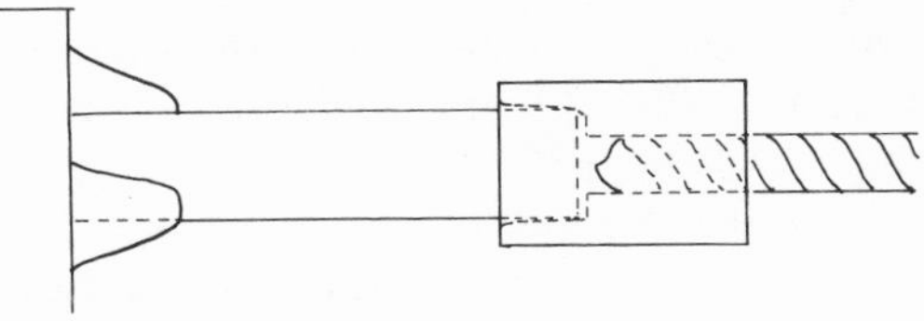

Fig. 5.2: Drill Guide

But there is no guarantee that a screw that you cut will fit; antiques often are not a standard size. One solution is to drill out the threaded hole and fit it with a threaded bushing, preferably something like nylon instead of metal, the size of the screw that you have made; I recommend that only an expert woodworker try this.

If you do not care to invest in a threading tap and die set, there is one alternative that *might* (cross your fingers and pray) work. *If* you're lucky you might find a lumberyard or hardware store that still carries build-your-own shelf units that use wooden screws to fasten turned wooden sections together. The company quit making them a couple of years ago and many retailers returned their stock. But you *may* find a store with a few leftovers and, if you are *very* lucky, the screws *might* fit. I have been lucky three times in over a hundred spinning wheels.

However you go about obtaining a proper sized screw, it should be spliced onto the handle, leg, etc., as mentioned above for broken legs.

The button on the end of the crank is a little easier to replace. First file the broken off stub off flat with the crank. Next take a 20d (20 penny common) nail and saw off a piece 5/8" (15.5mm) long from the head end. Drill a hole in the end of the crank using a #4 drill and silver-solder or braize the nail end in place. If the crank end is too narrow to accommodate a hole this size without being seriously weakened, make the hole 5/32" (3.9mm) and turn down a portion of the nail shank to fit. Turn it down before cutting off the 5/8" end. Put the turned down portion through the hole and rivet the back of it with a ball-peen hammer. The head of the nail becomes the new head on the crank. Be sure to smooth the back so that it does not catch on the footman as it goes around.

If the entire axle or crank needs replacing, you are best off finding a good weldor, blacksmith or tool and die maker. Take them the broken pieces and have a new axle and crank made.

One thing that I would warn against—using braizing on iron or steel parts. The braizing is a brass color and it sticks out like a sore thumb on steel parts. However if you are making the metal parts out of brass, then of course braizing is best. Or at least be very sparing with the solder.

If you are missing the entire spinning assembly, you should go to a spinning wheel restorer. You *can* do it yourself, if you've got a jig saw, a lathe and some hand tools. A drill press is also helpful. It's not too difficult to build, but getting it to fit properly is another matter. Naturally there is the distance between the maidens to consider. But the pulleys must also line up properly with the drive wheel, and the flyer must not extend beyond the end of the bobbin pulley or it will dislodge the drive band. In the case of some early American Saxony wheels, you must also be sure that the flyer will clear the drive wheel when the tension adjustment is loosened all the way. The bobbin must not rub on the flyer, and the flyer pulley should not rub on the rear maiden. The bobbin must be able to turn freely, and the pulleys must be the proper ratio to each other. Most important, you should be able to tell which kind of spinning assembly (double-pulley, bobbin-lead or flyer-lead) belongs on which kind of spinning wheel.

A missing flyer pulley also takes a restorer, or at least someone with a left-handed threading tap of the right size to match the thread on the spindle. Use this to thread a nut for the center of the replacement pulley. The hole in the center of the pulley should be the size of the spindle shaft, with the side of the hole nearest the maiden large enough to hold the metal nut. The nut should be a tight press fit, with a little epoxy cement for good measure. Be sure that the nut is perfectly centered and a proper fit before you cement it. Better yet, drill the center hole and cement the nut in place, then screw it onto a threaded metal rod (if you have the tap, you probably have the threading die) and use this for a center for turning the pulley. If you cannot get an exact match to the thread on the shaft, you might be able to re-thread the shaft to fit a certain size nut.

One way to make a bobbin if you have a double chuck lathe: start with a piece of 5/8″ (15.5mm) dowel rod cut to length. Clamp it in one chuck and clamp a drill bit the proper size for the hole in the other chuck and drill out the entire length of the dowel. You might have to take the piece out and turn it around; come at it from both ends. Use a drill one or two sizes larger than the shaft. Next take a ¾″ (2cm) thick board (birch is good) and rough out the bobbin ends on a jig or band saw. To turn the ends, my dad has made a 1½″ faceplate with a ¼″ (3mm) machine screw down the center. We drill a ¼″ hole in the center of the bobbin end and screw it to the faceplate. The faceplate is clamped in the lathe chuck and the bobbin end is turned. The end piece is then removed from the faceplate and (gently!) clamped in the lathe chuck. A 5/8″ (15.5mm) drill is then clamped in the tail chuck and the center of the bobbin is drilled out using the ¼″ hole as a pilot. This assures a perfectly centered, true running bobbin end.

If you don't have a double chuck or machinist's lathe, but you do have a wood lathe, start with a piece of 1″ (25mm) dowel rod cut to length, and drill the hole as straight and centered as you can. A drill press helps here. Next rough out the end pieces (be generous) and bore a 1″ hole in the center of each. Glue the ends on the piece of dowel. Put the rough bobbin in the lathe, *centering it carefully and accurately* on the drilled center hole. Then turn the entire bobbin, including the dowel. If it has been correctly centered on the hole, the entire bobbin will then run nice and true.

For how to make the flyer, see Chapter 4.

Once again let me point out that these repairs are better left to an expert repairman with a thorough knowledge of spinning wheels. If you have *any* doubts as to your ability, please take the spinning wheel to a restorer rather than try yourself, discover you can't, and then have to find an expert who will only have to undo what you've done. Now don't get me wrong. I do *not* think that everyone but me is a fumble-fingers! I have seen some surprisingly good amateur repair jobs, but I've also seen some real messes. The point that I'm trying to make is know your own limits. Know what you can do yourself, and when to seek an expert's help.

VI
RESTORATION

There is quite a difference between *repairing* a spinning wheel and *restoring* it. To repair something is to get it back in working order using whatever means necessary. To restore something is to return it as nearly as possible to original condition using the original methods of construction wherever you are able. I am a stickler for authenticity, with a special fondness for antique spinning wheels, so this chapter is my soap box. Those of you with modern spinning wheels may disregard this chapter.

It really pains me to see bungled repair jobs, beautiful antiques that some latter-day owner has varnished or painted, a spinning wheel turned into a lamp or planter, or an antique standing out on a porch or in a display window where the sun and rain are slowly destroying it. Part of my purpose in writing this book is an attempt to prevent such abuse.

Glue. Many antique spinning wheels, especially the more primitive ones, were never glued together. So glue has no place in restoration work unless something is cracked, split or broken. Or unless you can find evidence that the spinning wheel was glued originally. Loose legs and posts should be pegged, wedged and/or shimmed, not glued.

Screws and Nails. These likewise have no place in restoration work. Please! Do not drive a nail into the base of a loose post to secure it! And a treadle that's coming apart should be repegged, not nailed. Sometimes you do find a spinning wheel where nails have been used to secure loose posts. If the nails appear very old and rusted this may come under the heading of household repairs performed by some early owner to keep it running. If you try to pull the nail out and the head snaps off, then you *know* it's old! Even newer nails can be difficult to get out without gouging the wood. And sometimes repairs cannot be made without taking the spinning wheel apart. So *please* peg or shim! Pegs can be drilled out; nails can't!

Paint and varnish. Some East European spinning wheels were decoratively painted, and some Scandinavian and latter-day Canadian spinning wheels were painted completely. In fact, some Scandinavian spinning wheels will have two or three coats of paint; everytime the spinning wheel was handed down to a new bride, it was given a coat of paint to make it look new. With these exceptions, most antique spinning wheels were never given any sort of finish. The wood was just sanded or scraped smooth and left to acquire a patina through age and handling. Wood naturally darkens with age, and smoke from a fireplace would just add to this. Also, wool has a lot of natural grease in it, and a good deal of this was rubbed into the wood through the natural course of use. You will find that the tension screw handle is often the shiniest part, from the frequent handling it got.

Some latter-day owners acquiring a spinning wheel as a parlor ornament will give it a coat of varnish. This detracts from the value of an antique, and nothing looks tackier than a coat of cheap varnish improperly applied. If you want a nice finish that will both preserve and enhance the spinning wheel, try a penetrating oil like Watco. If your wheel has a clear finish that you think is original, it's more likely to be shellac than varnish, since shellac was more readily available. To match a clear finish with a reddish tone, try orange shellac, then dull the shine with fine steel wool.

Shims. There are some cases where a washer or shim is needed to take up space where a part has shrunk or become worn. I think that making these parts out of leather or wood is far more authentic than using cardboard, cloth or plastic, and certainly more durable.

Wood Putty. And as I've said before, please no wood putty or cellulose fiber wood fillers! Cracks can often be drawn together by gluing and clamping, and missing pieces of wood should be replaced with wood. I have a collection of worn out and broken parts that I use for lectures to illustrate various points about repairs. Among them is a bobbin that I can only describe as incredible. It was originally turned out of one block of wood, which was made by gluing two pieces of wood together. Later, the glue joint failed, causing about one third of the bobbin to split off. Instead of using glue and clamps, someone smeared both parts with wood putty and pressed them together. It holds, but it looks like a mess, and they compounded the problem by varnishing over it.

Now there are some cases where you have to use wood putty, but it should be done carefully. It must be well sanded and stained to match or it looks cheap and makeshift. There was an upright spinning wheel where the bench had split in several places and some wood was missing from the bottom. Someone had nailed strips of tin around the bench to hold it together – a rather makeshift household repair at best. I carefully glued the pieces together and then filled in the bottom with wood putty to reinforce it. But this was on the bottom where it wouldn't show. In the long run, in the interest of aesthetics I try to avoid wood putty altogether.

Documentation. One final word on restoration; document the work! Write down what was done to the spinning wheel, when and by whom. List any replacement parts. Save this as a record of the spinning wheel's authenticity. If the spinning wheel belongs to a museum, it is especially important to know how much of the spinning wheel is original. It's also important to have a record of who did the work in case it ever needs further care.

VII
MAKE IT YOURSELF

If your hobby is woodworking and you have already built some furniture, you might consider trying your hand at building a spinning wheel from scratch. It's a challenge, but if you have a good set of plans and you know wood and woodworking and you know how a spinning wheel operates, it's not difficult. This is how my father and I got started. I wanted to take up spinning but I couldn't find an antique spinning wheel and I couldn't afford a modern replica. My dad built my first spinning wheel for me, and he later built a yarn winder, a swift and a spinning chair to match. He says that my spinning wheel was the most woodturning that he ever did in one project.

You can build a spinning wheel by taking measurements from an existing wheel, but it's much easier, especially for a beginner, if you follow a set of blueprints. *Workbench Magazine* has printed blueprints for two styles of spinning wheels and a yarn winder. These are available from the magazine for the cost of a photostat. *Popular Mechanics* also printed plans for an upright spinning wheel, which were reprinted in their *Do-It-Yourself Encyclopedia.* My public library has the *Encyclopedia;* your's might too. If not, try writing the magazine. The *Foxfire Book #2* tells you how to build a wool wheel, a floor loom and a primitive yarn winder. Check any good bookstore or your public library. Craft Plans Company, Constantine's, Furniture Designs and Woodcraft Supply Corporation all have spinning wheel plans for sale, as do some spinning and weaving suppliers. I have listed as many of these as I can in the back of the book under "Sources", as well as further information on the above publications.

Once you have the plans, next comes selecting the wood. Any good hardwood will do. You can go as plain or as exotic as you like. You can make it traditional early American with oak for the bench, wheel rim and treadle (for strength) and a nice furniture wood such as maple or birch for the rest (for nice woodturning). Or you can make it solid cherry like a German upright that I worked on. Or solid walnut like an 1863 spinning wheel that my dad restored. Or pear wood with walnut ornamentation (light yellow with dark brown) like a French Tyrolean wheel that I restored. You can do like one spinning wheel builder who went to his son's farm, cut down a walnut tree, seasoned the wood for two years, and built spinning wheels from it. Or you can do like my dad who went to our local lumber yard and bought birch dowel rod and shelving; with fruitwood stain and satin finish varnish it looks like hand-rubbed early American maple. Let your imagination and your budget be your guide.

Making a nice looking spinning wheel is not hard, but making one that operates well is another story. Every spinning wheel builder should have a thorough knowledge of how a spinning wheel operates. The best way to go about this is to learn to spin on a borrowed or rented spinning wheel. This way you will be able to see and understand how and why the different parts work together the way they do. An alternative is to consult an experienced spinner for advice.

The spinning assembly is the most critical part of the spinning wheel. This must work correctly or the spinning wheel will not produce yarn. As I said before, if you are making a double-pulley spinning assembly the bobbin pulley should be at least ¼ smaller than the circumference of the flyer pulley. If they are too close in size you will not have an adequate pull to feed onto the bobbin. Also the bobbin must spin freely on the shaft and must not rub on the flyer.

The flyer has two sets of hooks, one on each arm for balance. When the orifice has two exit holes the hooks can be on opposite sides of the flyer. When there is only one exit hole both sets of hooks should be on the same side of the flyer; one for spinning and one for plying (Fig. 7.1). An easy way to make hooks is to take ¼″ (6mm) screw eyes and open them up with a pliers. If you want something larger, brass cup hooks work nicely. Check your local hardware store. Whatever you use, the end hooks on both ends of each side should feed the yarn on just inside the end of the bobbin. A spinning wheel designed for bulky yarn works well with hooks on 7/8″ centers (unless the spinning assembly is extra long), but finer yarns require ½″ centers. If you find that you've underestimated, you can always add more.

There is a relatively simple way to make the shaft and orifice for the spinning assembly (Fig. 7.2). Start with a piece of metal rod 3/16″ to 1/4″ (5mm to 6mm) in diameter. Measure from the inside edge of the front leather to the inside edge of the back leather and cut the rod to this length. Next, take a piece of metal tubing that has an inside diameter the same as the diameter of the rod; that is, a piece of tubing that will just fit over the rod. Take a drill bit slightly smaller than the inside of the tubing and drill a hole through the tubing. Or take a hack saw and cut a notch in the side of the tubing (see diagram). The edge of the hole should be 1/4″ to 3/8″ (6mm to 10mm) from the end of the tubing. Be sure to smooth the edges of the hole(s) inside

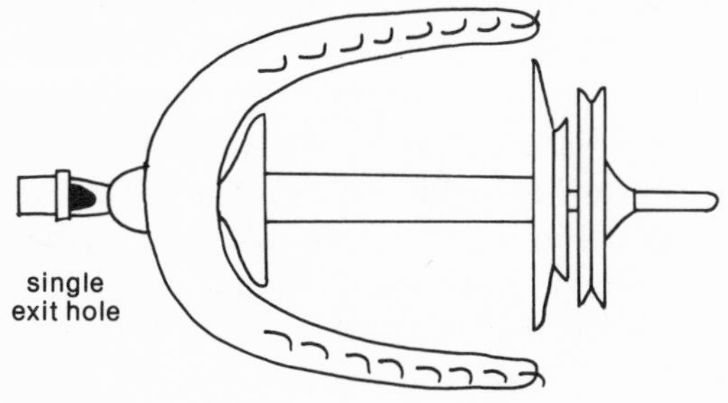

Hooks all on same side

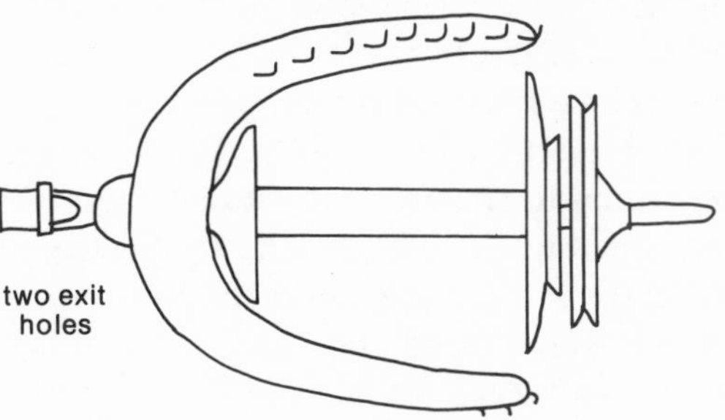

Hooks on opposite sides

Fig. 7.1

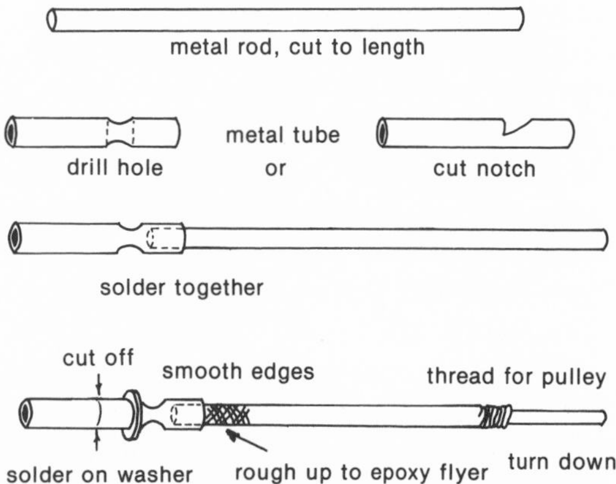

Fig. 7.2: Making a spinning assembly shaft.

and out, for these will be the exit holes in the spindle head. Also smooth the outside of the end of the tube. Slide the tube over the rod *up to* the hole and attach it. If you are using brass rod and tube, braize the joint or solder it carefully so that the solder doesn't show. If you are using iron or steel, braze carefully so it won't show, or solder or weld. Cut the tubing off ½" (12mm) from the other end of the hole and smooth the end inside and out. This will be the orifice. Next take a washer that will just fit over the tube and solder or braze it in place 1/8" (3mm) from the hole (see diagram). Next take a file and rough up the shaft just back of the tubing to give the epoxy cement something to hold to when you cement the flyer on, but do not put the flyer on permanently yet. Decide where the flyer pulley will go and thread the shaft. If you are using a set screw instead of a threaded nut, file a small flat or dent in the shaft for the set screw to hold on. Otherwise, every time the screw loosens the slightest bit the pulley will slip, and this can be very exasperating!

When threading the shaft it is important that the pulley does not go on so far that it is pressing tightly against the bobbin. The bobbin must be able to spin freely. When you have found where the pulley goes and cut the threads, put the shaft in a lathe and turn down the end to remove most of the threads not covered by the pulley when it is in place. Smooth the end and you are ready to add the wooden parts of the spinning assembly. For instructions on making a flyer see Chapter 4. Bobbins and pulleys are explained in Chapter 5. If you do not want to make a new front leather bearing for your spinning wheel, start with a piece of tubing that will fit the hole snugly but still turn freely and go from there. If you are making an oversized spinning assembly, you will want to adjust the above measurements accordingly.

The drive wheel of the spinning wheel is also very important; ideally, it is perfectly centered and lines up perfectly with the spinning assembly.

The wheel rim is usually made in four parts, with the wood grain running in a square like a picture frame. If your joints are a perfect fit, glue may be sufficient, but it's better to make a tongue-in-groove or splined joint, glue it, and cross-peg it (Fig. 7.3).

There is an even better way to build a wheel rim, especially if you want it to last the next five generations. Make the wheel rim in eight sections, two halves of four sections each (Fig. 7.4). Stagger the joints so that the joint on one side comes in the middle of the section on the other side. Use plenty of white glue and clamp it well, and you will have the sturdiest, most warp free, true running wheel rim you could want.

Regardless of what type of joint you use, you may run into the same problem that my dad had when he built my spinning wheel; our lathe will not take anything over 9″ in diameter and does not have an outboard faceplate capability. Well, necessity is the mother of invention. He turned the rim on the drill press. No, he did not clamp the wheel in the drill chuck and spin it. He took a piece of ½″ (12mm) plywood, mounted a metal rod in the center as a pivot, and clamped it to the table of the drill press. Another board with a hole for the pin sat on top of this (Fig. 7.5). The rim was fastened to the top board with finger clamps, which were mounted on the inside or outside of the rim as needed (Fig. 7.6). He put a router bit in the drill press, locked

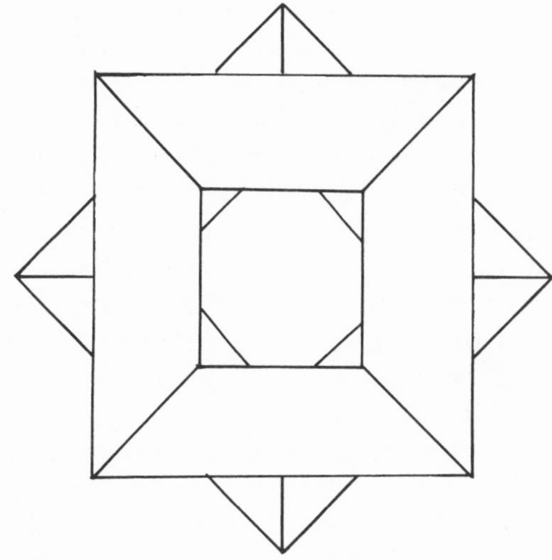

Fig. 7.4:
Wood sections glued together for eight-section rim. For four-section rim, rough out sections and join securely.

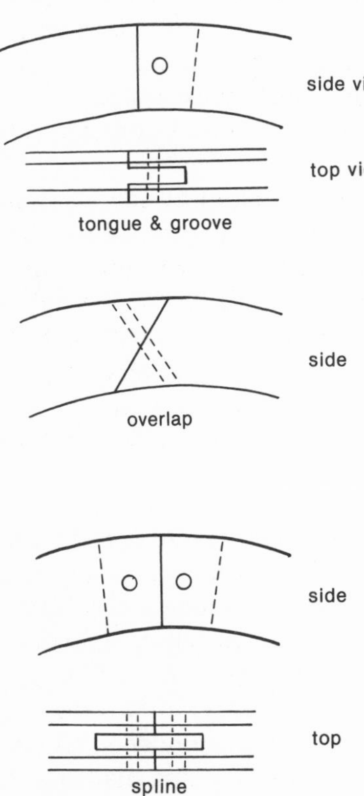

Fig. 7.3: Wheel rim joints

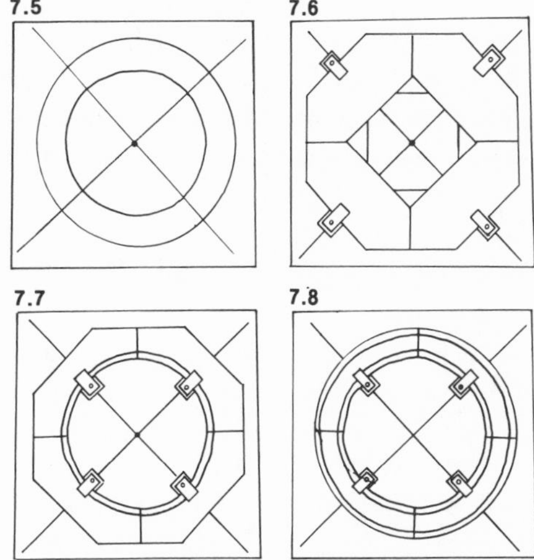

Fig. 7.5: Rim outlined on pivot board. **Fig. 7.6:** Rim roughed out and clamped to pivot board with finger clamps. **Fig. 7.7:** Inside of rim turned and finger clamps moved to the inside (place new clamps before removing old clamps). **Fig. 7.8:** Outside rim completed. Turn rim over, reclamp, and turn other side.

it at the proper depth, and used the two plywood boards as a turntable. It's slower and the finger clamps have to be moved several times (Figs. 7.7 and 7.8), but if you don't have the right sort of lathe it works rather nicely. You might have some trouble locating the right shape cutters for such things as the driveband grooves in the outside of the rim; some of the cutters Dad used I think he made himself. But it just shows that with a little ingenuity you can improvise anything.

Mounting the rim on the spokes and hub must be done carefully so that the rim will be perfectly centered. Turn the hub on the lathe and drill the spoke holes. Turn the spokes, mount them in the hub, and cut them off at length-plus-a-little. Take a piece of ½" plywood and mount a rod in the center for pivot, or take the bottom half of the pivot-board arrangement you used for turning the rim, and clamp it to the table of a disc or belt sander. We use a table saw with a sanding disc. The pivot board should be placed so that the ends of the spokes will brush the sanding disc or belt as the hub and spoke unit revolves on the pivot pin. As the hub is much thicker than the spokes, a small block of wood should be placed under the spoke to support it as it is being sanded. After all of the spokes have been sanded even, fit the hub and spoke unit in the rim. Too big? Sand some more. Keep sanding and fitting until you have a perfect fit, and then glue it in place. I would not rely on the glue alone, but would also peg the spokes. On many antique spinning wheels the inside of the wheel rim often had a ridge on one side or was tapered to make for a tight fit with the spoke unit, which was then pegged from the side to hold it securely. On small spinning wheels with narrow rims, the pegs were put in from the outside of the rim (Fig. 7.9).

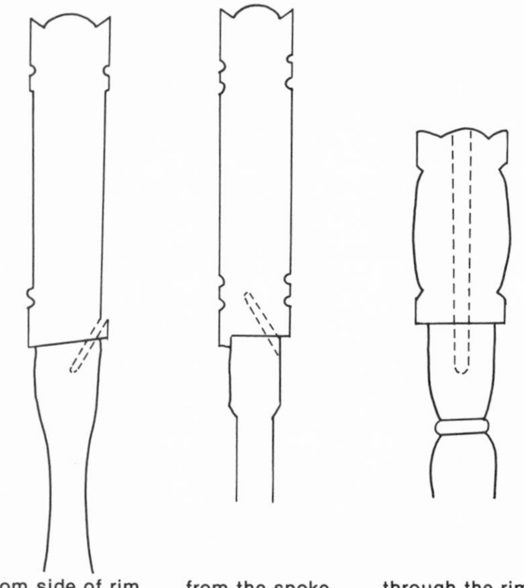

Fig. 7.9: Methods of pegging spokes to rim.

Proper action of the spinning assembly and proper alignment of this with the drive wheel are the most important points on a spinning wheel, but you should also be sure that all of the legs and posts fit securely. Don't just rely on glue; crosspeg everything that you can.

Like any artist, you will naturally want to sign your masterpiece. Go ahead! And put the date on it, too. The best place is the bottom side of the bench and the best method I've found is a woodburning pen. Too much spinning wheel history has been lost because so few craftsmen signed their work. Signing yours will also be a help to the family historian of some future generation of your descendents. An heirloom was originally something made on the loom for your heirs, but today this can apply to woodworking as well.

VIII FINISHING TOUCHES

This chapter deals with the appearance of your spinning wheel. I will tell you how to clean a spinning wheel, how to remove an old finish and apply a new one, and how to make new parts match the rest of the spinning wheel.

Finished or not, an antique spinning wheel will probably be dirty. So the first problem is cleaning it. First use a brush to remove loose dirt and cobwebs. If it's as bad as my mom's spinning wheel, which was covered with soot, you may want to go over it with a vacuum cleaner. After you've done this, or if the dirt is just rubbed in grease and grime, you go over the entire spinning wheel with #000 fine steel wool and plenty of "elbow grease" until you are down to the bare wood—or down to the paint or varnish, as the case may be. One wheel owner cleaned her wheel with something called Cotton Cleanser and it seemed to work pretty well. Flax soap is also okay, but too much water can damage wood and I feel that a dry method such as steel wool is best.

Once you have the dirt off you can tell what sort of finish you have underneath. If the spinning wheel is painted or varnished, study it carefully. If the varnish is almost completely worn off, or the paint is worn in places that get a lot of use such as the treadle, the paint could be original. Also take into consideration where the wheel is from. Scandinavian, East European and latter-day Canadian spinning wheels are more likely to have been painted than others. Remove the finish or not, as you please, but I would leave it if I thought it were original. DO NOT take it to one of these furniture stripping shops that dunks the piece in tanks of chemicals! The chemicals they use are too harsh and will leave the spinning wheel looking weathered and bleached. From a Norwegian wheel that was dunk stripped I learned that this soaking can also cause parts to swell or warp. I had to sand down all the joints before I could get this spinning wheel back together! And then I had to give it a coat of stain to hide the bleached look. So get a good paint stripper and do it yourself or get a friend to do it for you.

If you're going to strip it yourself, you'll need a nice warm day or two, and some shade to work in. It's best to work outdoors, but if you must work inside be sure that you have generous ventilation. Several open windows and an exhaust fan are a good idea. Be sure to read all of the warnings and directions on the paint stripper can. Most of these strippers are rather caustic so it's a good idea to wear rubber gloves. Your work surface should be at a comfortable height. I use an old picnic table. Some boards or a sheet of plywood on two sawhorses also works well. Whatever you use, be sure to cover it well with newspapers to protect the surface and make cleanup easier. Different brands of stripper may work differently, but generally you paint the stripper on, wait about five minutes, and scrape off the softened

PAINT
STRIPPER

finish with a putty knife. Then paint on another thin coat of paint stripper, wait, and scrub it off with steel wool dipped in a solution of water and tri-sodium-phosphate. I use a Brillo pad instead of the TSP. Be sure not to get the wood too wet. Use a well-rung-out sponge to remove the soap and excess moisture.

This is a messy, time consuming and sometimes frustrating job. But it's well worth the bother. The natural wood, enhanced by wax, is a thing of beauty. My Swiss upright wheel was originally a blond color, with a thin coat of varnish. Some time between being sold to an antique importer and ending up in the antique shop where I found it, someone slopped (and I mean SLOPPED!) a coat of dark brown stain over it to "antique" it. It took me two weekends, a can of paint stripper and some four letter words to get it off, but I'm glad I did. Most parts of the wheel were fairly well protected by the varnish (which came off with the stripper), but in some areas it soaked into the wood. So I gave the wheel a light coat of light brown stain to blend and camouflage the uneven color, and then a coat of paste wax. A big improvement.

If you do take the spinning wheel to a dunk-and-strip place, or if your spinning wheel has had water damage (flooded basement?), or if it's like one spinning wheel I restored that had sat out in the wood shed exposed to the weather for who-knows-how-long, it will be badly bleached, stained and/or weathered. It will need careful work before it is ready for finishing. First clean it thoroughly with steel wool, even if it's not noticeably dirty. This will smooth down the roughness of the wood and remove or blend stain lines. Next, find a color of wood stain that you feel is the color the spinning wheel should be or that matches the undamaged areas. Avoid stain-finish or stain-sealer. And *please* don't use stain-varnish; it looks cheap. Just a plain oil or water-base stain. I prefer the oil base, myself. You might want to test it on a not too noticeable part of the spinning wheel like under the bench to see what color you will come out with. Old wood, especially bleached or weathered, will soak up the stain very quickly. So instead of painting it on and wiping the excess off, I put some on a rag and lightly rub it on the spinning wheel. This way you can control the color and shading more easily. If the color isn't dark enough you can go over it again, but it's very difficult to remove color if you get it too dark.

I find that most stains seem to be yellow-browns, red-browns or grey-browns. The colors that I seem to use most are fruitwood, cherry, Danish walnut, dark oak and mahogany. If you want a pale yellow-brown like new wood, try pecan or English oak. Sometimes you have to use a combination—one stain over another—to get the right shade.

I've done a lot of color matching and I can look at a spinning wheel and say, "That looks like fruitwood" or "This looks like mahogany base with walnut shading." You'll just have to experiment. When you are trying to match new parts to old, you can often test the colors on a scrap of the same kind of wood first. Also, keep in mind that most antiques are not all the same shade. Grooves and crevices are sometimes darker than smooth areas, and the axle areas will often be stained black by years of lubricating. A few careful dents and nicks will often blend a new piece in with the old.

Staining a new spinning wheel is not as complicated, of course. You should make sure that the spinning wheel is well sanded and that the wood is free of grease and oil. I'd be sure that I had enough stain to do the entire spinning wheel. If you run out half-way through you may end up with a two-tone wheel. One other point; it doesn't hurt to assemble the spinning wheel first to be sure that all the parts will fit properly, then take it apart and stain it.

When your spinning wheel is completely stripped, cleaned and, if necessary, stained, then comes the final step; applying a finish to seal and protect the spinning wheel. Most antique spinning wheels were never given any sort of a finish, but having survived this long they generally need something to help preserve them. My favorite is paste wax. A good paste wax such as Johnson's or Minwax will enhance the color and grain of the wood and give it a lovely warm sheen. For best results apply a thin coat of wax and let it harden overnight. Then polish. I find that an old terrycloth towel does a wonderful job of polishing. If your spinning wheel is especially dried out, you may need two or three coats of wax. Apply it until it stops soaking into the wood.

Stay away from boiled linseed oil as a finish unless you're prepared to put a lot of energy into the job. Done properly, it requires sparing application and lots of vigorous hand rubbing to build up friction heat and harden the oil. Done the way most people use it (wipe it on and let it soak in), it just dulls the finish and collects dust. It also rubs off easily and has a distinct odor. If you want to use an oil finish, and for badly dried out spinning wheels this is sometimes best, use a penetrating oil or a lemon oil/beeswax mixture.

For finishing a modern spinning wheel you can use anything you want. I sometimes use paste wax, but there are many good varnishes out on the market that are better as a wood preservative. You can get satin finish varnish for a lovely hand-rubbed sheen, or gloss finish varnish which is just what the name implies; glossy. Both of these also come in a polyurethane formula which resists waterspots and stains, and a quick-drying formula for those in a hurry. Be sure that the spinning wheel is thoroughly sanded smooth or you will end up with a finish that feels like the sandpaper. Brush on one coat sparingly with a clean brush. When this is thoroughly hardened rub it down lightly with fine sandpaper, clean carefully, and sparingly apply a second coat of varnish. If this is not enough you can always give it another coat, but drips and runs from too much varnish are unsightly. And do not do any dusting or sanding in the area until the varnish is dry or you will find all the dust sticking to the wet varnish. To keep your spinning wheel looking nice, give it an occasional going over with a good furniture polish.

IX
GREASE JOB

It's no use having a spinning wheel in beautiful shape if you don't take care of it. A spinning wheel is a piece of machinery, not furniture, and as such it needs maintenance. When I'm giving a lecture I like to tell the story of the time I was demonstrating spinning at an arts and crafts fair. There was also a woman there demonstrating spinning for a Revolutionary War group (this was the Bicentennial) and when she heard that there was another spinner present, she came over to say hello and see what I was doing. She was admiring my spinning wheel and I let her try it. She was surprised at how easily mine treadled and complained that hers was very stiff. I asked her what she was using to grease it with. "Grease? You mean I'm supposed to grease it?"

Unfortunately, the story is very true. Moving parts need lubrication. It is assumed that everyone knows this and very little is said on the subject. Spinning books that do mention lubrication usually include only a brief paragraph or two. But lubrication is necessary to prevent excessive wear and to make the spinning wheel work easier.

So next comes the question, what do you use? And here the confusion starts. Some books recommend powdered graphite. Others say to use paraffin (candle wax). Many people are inclined to reach for the oil can. Others use grease. My dad tried silicone spray and someone else recommended WD-40 to me. So which is correct? Answer: all of the above, except graphite (too messy) and silicone (doesn't do any good). The secret is in knowing what to use where.

The general guideline is that non-porous surfaces need oil and porous surfaces need grease (actually, grease *is* oil, with a thickener such as mineral soap added). Rough surfaces need paraffin.

To break that down a bit: if both surfaces are nonporous (metal or nylon) then the lubricant will not soak in and will stay where it's put, so you can use oil, preferably mineral oil or a 30 wt. motor oil. If *one or both* of the surfaces are a highly porous material (wood or leather) you will have to use grease, as oil will just soak in and not stay where it's needed. You also have to use grease for plastic surfaces, as this material resists oil. The American pioneers used a mixture of pinetar and lard for axle grease for their wagons, and it's entirely possible that the lady of the house would use a little of this on her spinning wheel from time to time. Or maybe she used mutton tallow. Nowadays, if you can't get axle grease from your friendly neighborhood garage mechanic, use petroleum jelly (Vaseline).

The tension screw, at least on the old spinning wheels and on the less expensive modern wheels, is wood on wood. For two such rough surfaces, grease won't do much good. So if you have a sticking tension screw, rub it with paraffin and work it through the hole a couple of times.

WD-40 is a petroleum-based lubricant that comes in an aerosol can. It can be used anywhere that you would use oil. The advantage to using it is that the can comes with a long thin nozzle that fits into hard-to-reach places. The disadvantage is that being an aerosol, you tend to get too much too quickly and after the solvent evaporates, less lubricant is left behind than you probably want. Also, without the nozzle, it tends to go all over the place.

So the next question is: where do you lubricate? The most obvious place is the wheel axle. On a conventional Saxony wheel and on most upright wheels, you can just take a toothpick and put a generous dab of grease in the slot on top of the axle. On some spinning wheels, you might have to pull a pin out of the wheel hub and slide the axle part way out. Rub grease on the axle and slide it back in place, twisting it back and forth as you do so. The upright wheel that my dad made me also lacked wheel axle slots (Dad thought the upright posts would be stronger this way), and I got fed up with having to take it apart every time I wanted to lubricate it. So he put grease-fittings on it (Fig. 9.1). He made two metal thumb screws to match the rest of my spinning wheel, and then drilled a hole in the side of each post going into the axle hole. The hole is filled with grease using a toothpick and the screw is twisted into place, forcing the grease into the axle area. Excess grease works its way to the outside end of the axle and can be wiped off.

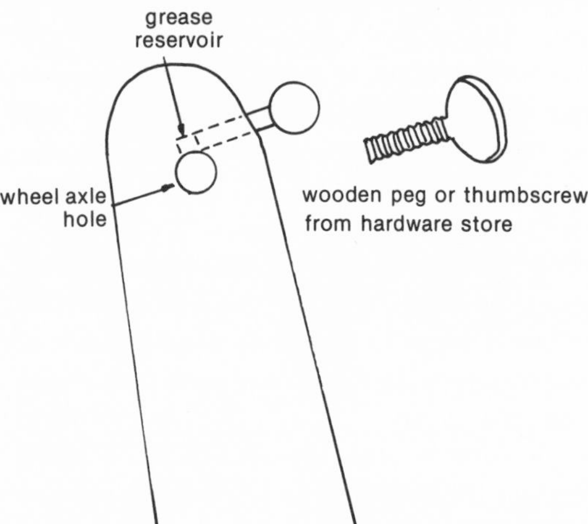

Fig. 9.1: Greasefitting (shown on Ashford Wheel)

Unless they are grease-packed and "sealed for life", the ball bearings on modern wheels should be oiled.

The second most important spot to lubricate is the spinning assembly axle points. Remove the spinning assembly, or at least slide it part way out, and rub the axle points liberally with grease. Slide it back in place, twisting it as you go. Again, if your spinning wheel has metal or nylon bearings use oil, not grease.

If your bobbins are not fitted with oil specific bearings, grease is the correct lubricant. Re-grease or oil frequently to keep the dirt swabbed out—one of the functions of lubrication on any part of your wheel.

Two other points that need lubrication are where the footman rests on the wheel crank and the treadle pivot pins.

If you have a hinged treadle, the leather hinges must be kept soft and flexible. They should be oiled once a year, even if the spinning wheel is not used much. Neetsfoot oil is the best, as it's specially made for softening leather. Just wipe a little on each hinge and let it soak in. On most spinning wheels the treadle is fastened to the footman with a leather thong. If your spinning wheel has a leather hinge here, like the Ashford, this should also be oiled.

After you have your spinning wheel thoroughly lubricated, treadle it a while to work in the grease or oil. You will notice that the excess will work its way to the outside of the axles. Be sure to wipe this off, and don't lean the spinning wheel against you when you carry it or, like myself, you will find yourself washing grease and oil out of your clothes. And I can tell you, scrubbing black grease out of a down-filled ski jacket is no fun.

Logically, the next question is: how often to lubricate your spinning wheel? This all depends on how often you use it. To prevent wear and keep your wheel in top condition, you should use a few drops of oil on every lubricating point every time you sit down to use it—and every hour thereafter. Don't wait until it becomes stiff or starts to squeak, any more than you would your car.

If you have a new spinning wheel with leather bearings, or if you have replaced an old bearing, it will need breaking in. The friction will liquify the grease and it will soak into the leather until it becomes saturated. So you will have to grease it often; at least once every couple hours with heavy use.

If you have an expensive modern spinning wheel that does not have the traditional leather bearings, it's a good idea to check the manufacturer's instructions on lubricating. I saw a lovely modern reproduction wool wheel being used at the Ozark Mountain Museum in Mountain Home, Arkansas. The woman using it told me that the wheel hub ran on ball bearings, and that the man who built it came in once a year to check it over and lubricate it. This is a rather unusual case, of course. You shouldn't have any problems if you follow the guidelines I've given you and use some common sense.

X
HELP! IT WON'T WORK!

Here at last is the chapter you've all been waiting for; what to do if your spinning wheel won't behave. Here are the solutions. I must warn you though, that about half the difficulties are problems with the spinner, not the spinning wheel. I advocate learning to spin on a drop spindle, and learning to treadle without spinning, then putting it all together on a spinning wheel. It's much easier. So practice a bit, and if you're still having trouble, read on.

Yarn overtwists. Overtwist is when the yarn starts to kink or knot up even under tension or where it repeatedly snaps at thin spots, and it's the most common beginner problem. Usually the spinner is holding the yarn back too long or treadling too fast. Often it's a combination of both. First, slow down your treadling as much as possible yet still keep the wheel going. Next, draw the fibers out faster and let them feed in as soon as they're drawn out. The moment you've drawn out one bunch of fibers, come back and pull out some more. Don't pause in between. Don't worry about lumps. Just make yarn. As you become more adept you can take time to perfect your yarn.

Another cause of overtwist is that the yarn is not feeding in fast enough. Try tightening the tension adjustment (move the spinning assembly further away from the drive wheel). On an Ashford wheel, tighten the bobbin brake band or loosen the flyer drive band.

Yarn won't feed in at all. First tighten the tension. If this doesn't work, check to see that the yarn is not caught on a hook or too thick to fit through the orifice. Sometimes this can be remedied by giving it a sharp pull out and then letting it feed in again. If it feeds in and jams again, it's too thick. If the tension is tight and the yarn is not caught, then you may have an insufficient ratio between the two pulleys. The best solution for this is to have the bobbin pulley groove cut deeper or a new flyer pulley made. A temporary solution is to put both drive bands on one pulley and tie the other pulley down to the mother-of-all. This converts a double-pulley spinning assembly into a bobbin-lead or flyer-lead spinning assembly (Fig. 10.1).

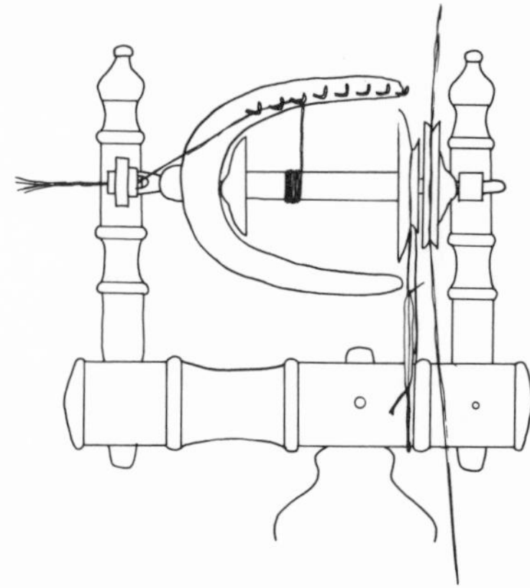

Double pulley spinning assembly converted to flyer-lead. Brake band on bobbin tied down to mother-of-all, incorporating rubberband for tension. Drive band on flyer pulley. For bobbin-lead, reverse the band positions.

Fig. 10.1

Yarn undertwists. If your yarn repeatedly pulls apart, then it's undertwisted. Undertwist is often caused by not holding the yarn back long enough for it to build up sufficient twist to hold. Don't let the spinning wheel pull the yarn away from you, hang onto it! Show it who's boss!

Too strong a feed-on. If the yarn is being pulled away from you and you can't hold it back, loosen the tension (move the spinning assembly closer to the wheel). On an Ashford wheel loosen the brake band on the bobbin. If this doesn't work, check the bobbin pulley to see if there is dirt or old grease in the groove that could be causing the drive band to stick. Or you might have the same problem that I sometimes have. I let the bobbin get too full near the pulley end and the yarn spills over into the pulley groove. The driveband will not slip on the yarn and all of a sudden the spinning wheel will "grab". Slip the drive band off the bobbin pulley, unwind the yarn until the bobbin pulley is clear, and then wind the yarn back on at a different spot on the bobbin. Slip the drive band back on and continue spinning.

To loosen the yarn pull on a bobbin-lead spinning assembly, loosen the tension on the drive band. On a flyer-lead, loosen the bobbin brake-band.

Yarn keeps breaking. This is usually a result of overtwist (the yarn finds a thin spot and snaps), or undertwist (not enough twist to hold the yarn together). Occasionally you find a spinning wheel where the edges of the orifice are sharp and keep cutting the yarn. Smooth the edges down with a round file and/or emery paper.

Wheel keeps reversing direction. You would swear that the wheel is being obstinate, but the truth of the matter is that you just need more practice treadling. On most spinning wheels, your heel is the pivot point and your toe pushes. As the wheel crank comes over the top of its circle you give it a shove, and then coast with it down, around and over the top where you give it another shove. If you are still pushing when the crank reaches the bottom of the circle, the wheel will stop or reverse direction (Fig. 10.2).

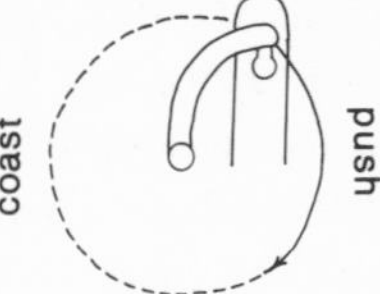

Wheel crank, as you face it to work.

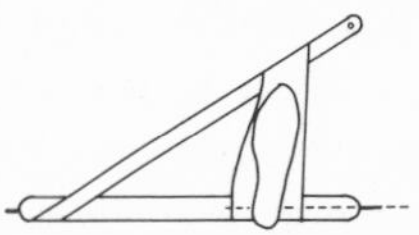

Fig. 10.2: Toe-control treadling action

On some modern wheels and some very small antique upright wheels, the pivot point of the treadle comes in the middle of the foot. You treadle with a toe-and-heel action similar to a treadle sewing machine. This is used where a smoother treadle action is desired or where the wheel is very small and light and doesn't have enough momentum to come back to the starting point by itself (Fig. 10.3).

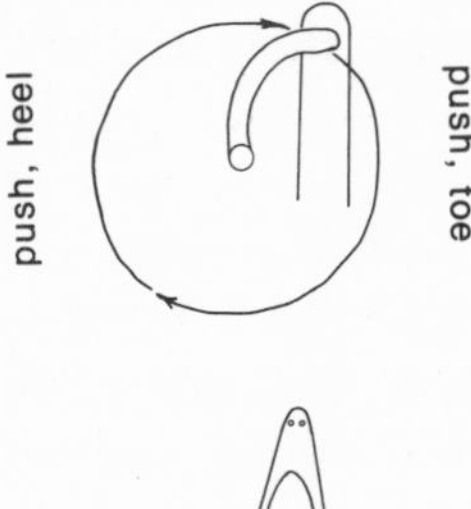

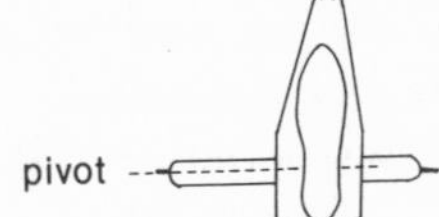

Fig. 10.3: Heel-toe treadling action

Footman rattles or jumps off. You probably have your foot too far back on the treadle. This means that you are tipping the treadle up with your foot and causing the treadle to bump the footman. With the exception of spinning wheels that are designed for a heel-and-toe action, your heel should be over the pivot bar. You won't have this problem with a hinged treadle unless the treadle is hitting the floor every time it goes around. If this is the case, either the tie-up or the footman is too long and needs to be shortened.

Band slips. This can be caused by wax, furniture polish or too much varnish in the wheel or pulley grooves making them too slippery. Use alcohol (solvent or rubbing) or turpentine to cut the wax. *Caution:* this could damage a varnished finish. Or you could clean the grooves with steel wool, sandpaper or a fine grade triangular or knife-edged file.

Another cause of band slippage is making the band out of the wrong material. Nylon is strong, but it's much too elastic. Cotton or linen cord works much better. Don't use something too narrow, either. I like a #12 seine twine, sometimes sold in hardware stores as chalk line. An 8 or 10 ply soft cotton twine will require less tension and thus less treadling effort; it will wear out faster, though, so you should keep a replacement handy. Loosen the tension all the way (move the spinning assembly as close to the wheel as possible) before you put a new band on. Otherwise you will have trouble with the band later on as it stretches out. The best thing for a double-pulley spinning assembly wheel is a single band that goes around twice rather than two separate bands. The band on the larger (flyer) pulley must cross outside of the band on the smaller (bobbin) pulley or else the bands will rub on each other. This causes the band to wear out faster, and sometimes to jump off (see below).

If you can splice the ends of the band together, beautiful! I can't, so I overlap the ends of the band and sew them together for about an inch (Fig. 10.4). Overcast up one side and down the other, being sure to wrap the ends well to keep them from fraying. Cut the ends of the cord off as close to the wrapping as possible. This makes a nice smooth joint that won't wear out as fast as a knot will. It also fits better in the rather narrow pulley grooves on some antique

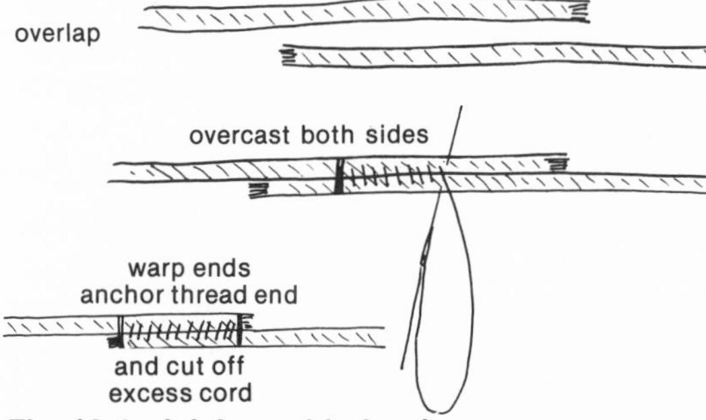

Fig. 10.4: Joining a driveband

spinning wheels. If you must tie a knot (i.e., for a temporary repair during a demonstration) use a square knot, surgeon's knot or fisherman's knot (Fig. 10.5). These will lie as flat and smooth as any knot can.

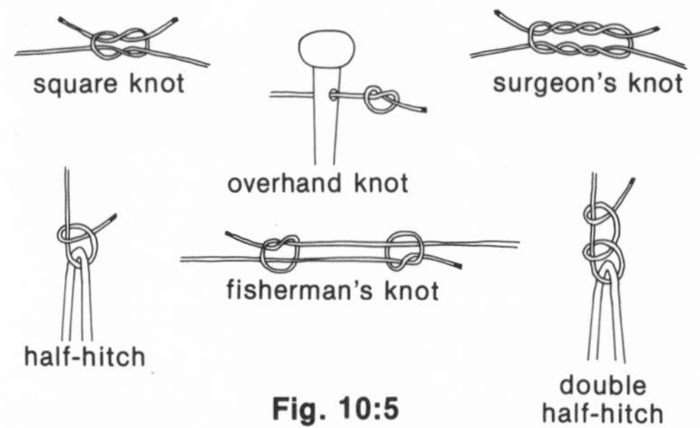

Fig. 10:5

Band jumps off. This can be one of the most annoying problems, and it seems that it usually happens when someone is watching you. There can be a number of causes for this. If it happens when you start your spinning wheel, check to see *how* you are starting it. If you give the rim a shove with your hand, you could be knocking the drive band off when you do. It's better for the drive band (and for the wheel rim) to catch a spoke with your finger to start the wheel turning.

If the front wheel peg is missing, the axle will hop about in the slot, throwing the wheel out of line and sometimes dumping the drive band off. Be sure that there is a sturdy peg in place and that the axle slot is not so badly worn that the axle hops even when the peg is in place.

If the drive band is improperly crossed (see above) the bands will rub and sometimes jump off. To recross a drive band (Fig. 10.6) you will need an area of empty floor or a large table and no interruptions.

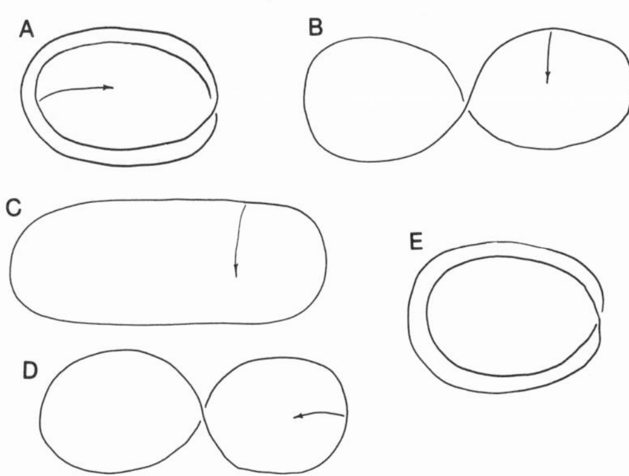

Fig. 10.6: Recrossing a driveband

Remove the drive band by removing the wheel and spinning assembly. Remember how it came off; which way you faced and which is top and bottom. Lay it flat on the table or floor (Fig. A). Open it up sideways to form a figure "8" (Fig. B). Bring one side of the band up or down to form an oval (Fig. C) and repeat the motion to form another figure "8" (Fig. D). Reverse Fig. B and fold the figure "8" over to form a double circle (Fig. E). Replace the band exactly the same way you took it off and you should find that the band is now properly crossed. For spinning clockwise, the band is set up one way. If you change directions the cross will move over to the other side of the wheel and the band will rub. If you are going to be doing much work going counter-clockwise or if the drive band won't stay on, the band should be recrossed. After you've done it a few times, you'll find that it's not as complicated as it sounds.

Tying a knot in the driveband can also cause problems. The knot may catch where the drive bands cross and cause the band to jump off. The drive band may also jump off if it's too thick to fit in the grooves. A #12 seine twine seems to be the right size for most any spinning wheel I've ever worked with. Another spinner I know swears by Japanese kite string. It seems to work okay for her, but I'll stick with my seine twine, thank you.

Spinning wheel works stiffly. Lubricate it (see Chapter 9). You'd be surprised what a difference a little grease can make. If you have a new spinning wheel and lubricating it doesn't seem to help, check to see that the axle, spindle and treadle holes line up properly with each other and that parts are not rubbing on each other. Also, some new spinning wheels need a little breaking in. Usually though, the problem is lubrication.

Spinning wheel squeaks. As the old saying goes, "The squeaky wheel gets the grease." See Chapter 9.

Spinning wheel creeps away from you. A very common and modern problem. Many antique spinning wheels had a metal spike in the bottom of the back leg that would dig into the floor and keep it from scooting away. With modern linoleum and varnished wood floors we have to find another solution. A number of spinners place a small throw rug under their spinning wheels. This works only if the rug has a rubber backing, or if you put your chair (and you) on the other end of the rug to anchor it. A rag rug by itself will slip worse than the spinning wheel will. One person I know uses a sheepskin, leather side down, which stays put and looks very appropriate. I found that a rubber (not plastic) furniture caster cup under the back leg worked very well. Except that I would lose too many of them at demonstrations when I would pack up my spinning wheel and go home and forget to pack the caster cup! So I now use the modern equivalent of the metal spike; a small half-round rubber bumper mounted on the bottom of the back leg. It works beautifully. A rubber crutch tip works well too if you're not fussy about appearance.

Wheel rocks as you spin. Your spinning wheel might have a loose leg, but more likely it's your padded carpeting. An upright wheel will rock more than a Saxony wheel will because it has a smaller leg span. I've learned to live with it, but if it bothers you, you can place a piece of plywood or hardboard under your wheel. Or move it to another room. What I sometimes find myself doing when I don't want the movement of the spinning wheel to cut down on my speed is to have one foot on the treadle of my upright and my other foot on the bench of the wheel to brace it. It sounds a little odd, but it works for me (when I'm barefoot). To each his own.

XI
PREVENTIVE MEDICINE

HOW TO GET IT THERE UNBROKEN

Getting your spinning wheel from one place to another without damaging it can create problems. Such as how to get your average early American Saxony wheel into your average two-door sedan. I had one spinning wheel brought in for repair with ten broken spokes and a broken treadle. The broken spokes were why it had been brought for repair. The owner broke the treadle getting it into her car. Another spinning wheel owner was a little more careful. She had a family heirloom Austrian Tyrolean wheel that was falling apart. Also, her dog had chewed up one corner of the base. She took the entire spinning wheel apart and very carefully wrapped each part in newspaper and masking tape and packed it all in a box. She did a very thorough job; she could have sent it Parcel Post safely. She took it to a spinning and weaving supply shop and the shop called their repairman (me). She had to have an estimate before I took it home to work on. So there I was, sitting on the floor in the middle of the shop, unwrapping packages like Christmas morning! And then there was another spinning wheel recently that was in such sad shape that the owner just gathered all the pieces together in a plastic garbage bag and brought them over. So in the interest of preserving your spinning wheel (and your sanity) and preventing unnecessary repair work, here are a few travel tips.

In most cases you will be traveling by car to lessons, meetings, demonstrations, workshops, craft fairs, etc. Naturally, the best sort of vehicle is a van or station wagon, but don't get discouraged if all you have is a compact. I can get three spinning wheels, supplies and myself into my Volkswagen beetle comfortably. It's just a matter of knowing how.

The upright spinning wheel was also known as the visiting wheel for an obvious reason; it was very compact and easy to cart around. And that's as true today as it was long ago. This type of spinning wheel will lay on its side on the back seat of a car very nicely, or can sometimes be stood up on the front passenger's seat. I can get two upright wheels or an upright and a small Saxony in the back seat, with or without folding the seat down. Even my mom's rather large Saxony and my upright will fit together if the Saxony is put in first.

A Saxony wheel usually travels best if stood on the back seat. If the Saxony is very large, or if your car ceiling is low, you may have to remove the drive wheel to get the spinning wheel to stand upright. This is usually a matter of removing two pegs, unhooking the footman and lifting the wheel out. Don't worry about the drive band becoming mixed up or re-crossed. Unless the spinning assembly comes out as well, the band will straighten itself out when you put it back on the wheel. But first, try putting the spinning wheel in the car without removing the wheel. You'd be surprised which cars will fit and which won't. Mom's Saxony can stand upright on the back seat of my beetle, but not in the back of Dad's full-sized Ford sedan.

The procedure that I find works best is to stand at the passenger's door holding the spinning wheel by the bench with it facing you as you would for spinning. Tip the low end of the bench up and fit the two shorter legs through the door. Then tip the high end up as you (carefully!) maneuver the wheel through the door, followed by the high end of the bench and the tall leg. Remember, wheel rims chip easily, especially when banged against door frames. Lean the spinning wheel toward you slightly to get the back leg in the back of the seat (be careful there's no metal spike in the leg to rip the upholstery) and stand the wheel upright on the seat. If the shorter legs have too great a span to both fit on the seat, rest the spinning wheel carefully on the treadle bar. Then fasten the seat belt. I'm not kidding! Use the seat belt to strap the spinning wheel in securely. Do this no matter what kind of spinning wheel you have or how you've packed it. This will keep the spinning wheel from shifting around when you turn corners and protect it from getting banged up if you have to stop suddenly. In *any* sort of maneuver you should have both hands on the steering wheel, not reaching out to catch a spinning wheel. Also if the leg splay is too great to fit on the seat, the seat belt will take some of the strain off the treadle bar.

If you are transporting your spinning wheel in the trunk, a Saxony should be stood upright if at all possible. An upright or a Saxony that is too large or too unsteady should be carefully laid on its side. Be sure that it is not resting on the mother-of-all, maidens, wheel rim or any other delicate part that can become loosened or broken. And it's a good idea to pad your spinning wheel with an old blanket or throw rug to protect it from nicks and scratches. The same goes for spinning wheels in hatchbacks. With vans, station wagons and pick-up trucks the spinning wheel should be laid on its side. Either that, or sit your assistant in the back to hold onto it every time you turn a corner.

Wool wheels are a different story. How do you transport something that big? Generally you don't, at least not the way you would cart a smaller spinning wheel around to every meeting and demonstration you go to. But there will be occasions when you have to get it from one place to another. The key word is "carefully". Don't try to force it through small doors and don't let it get banged around.

Most wool wheels disassemble rather easily, so the biggest problem is the wheel itself. Several years ago, I had to bring a wool wheel home from a local museum to do some restoration on it. At the time, I owned a VW Squareback (a small station wagon). The body of the spinning wheel fit inside the car well enough, but the wheel itself was wider than the car was! I ended up tying the wheel to the roof, a method that I do not recommend. To bring it back to the museum, we stood it up in the back of my brother-in-law's pick-up truck. A guaranteed traffic stopper if ever there was one. This is okay for short trips (if the weather's good) but it could be awkward for any great distance. The best way would be to stand it upright in a van with someone to steady it, or lay it flat in a station wagon. A friend of mine was able to fit her wool wheel in her two-door sedan by taking it apart. She fit the wheel through the door at an angle and lifted it up over the back of the front seat. The wheel rested on the front seat backs and the rear shelf. You might also be able to fit a small wool wheel in a four-door sedan by standing the wheel portion on edge on the floor of the back seat.

I haven't quite had a spinning wheel left on my doorstep, but one did arrive in a laundry basket. Movers had taken the spinning wheel apart to pack it and the owner didn't know how to get it back together again. If you are moving or if you have to take your spinning wheel with you on a train or airplane, it's best to pack it (yourself!) as you would for shipping. First disassemble the spinning wheel as much as you can. With a new spinning wheel you should be able to break it down into manageable-size components. To be sure that you get it back together correctly, it's a good idea to label all the parts. You can pencil corresponding numbers on the inside of a hole and the portion of the post that fits in it, or you can tie tags on the posts and their holes. Post A goes in hole A, leg #2 goes in hole #2, etc. It's also helpful to take some pictures of your spinning wheel while it's still in one piece so you'll know if you've got it together correctly. Next find a sturdy carton or crate that will hold all the parts with room for padding. Keep in mind that if you are shipping it via United Parcel Service, the circumference plus the length cannot exceed 108 inches. Other shippers may have similar size regulations.

Next comes the actual packing. The legs and wheel posts can be rolled in blank newsprint to protect the finish. The mother-of-all, maidens and support post can sometimes be left assembled but should be removed from the bench by removing the tension screw. On some spinning wheels you will have to drive a peg out of the bench before the tension screw will come out. Wrap well in paper for protection. Ideally, the spinning assembly should be packed in a box of its own within the carton. If this isn't possible, wrap it well in newspapers. The footman can usually be folded flat against the treadle. The wheel axle must be protected from getting bent if the carton gets dropped or squashed. You also have to keep the axle from poking through the side of the carton. To do this, you have to place something as thick as the axle is long on each side of the wheel. The wrapped legs and wheel posts serve this purpose well. An alternative is to cut two or three inch wide strips of corrugated cardboard, cut across the grain. Bend these into squares and tape or tie them to the sides of the wheel, surrounding the axles. Then tape, or better yet tie, all the parts together into a compact bundle. Write the destination and return address clearly on a piece of paper and attach it to the bundle "just in case". Fit this in the carton and fill any empty space well with crumpled newspaper. If you can get some styrofoam "popcorn" instead it will cut down somewhat on the weight. Tape and tie the box securely. With a waterproof black marker clearly print the return address and destination on the box. With a red marker print FRAGILE in large letters on all sides. And don't forget insurance. I'd figure the value of the spinning wheel and round the figure off to the next $50 and insure for this amount. It's worth it.

Never trust movers to pack a spinning wheel. Do it yourself. One spinner whom

I'd restored a spinning wheel for moved from Chicago to Tennessee. The movers broke part of her spinning wheel; I think it was the flyer and one of the maidens. She complained to the moving company and they said they'd fix it. She told them, "Oh no you don't! This is a valuable antique and it takes a specialist to fix it properly!" She shipped the broken parts back to me, and then sent the moving company a bill for the repairs and the shipping.

One word of advice on shipping a spinning wheel; I'd go with a commercial carrier such as United Parcel Service rather than trust U.S. Parcel Post. If UPS won't take your package, you might consider bus freight. Both Greyhound and Trailways take packages. If you don't mind paying more there are the air freight companies. However, if you're shipping overseas I think you'll have to rely on the U.S. Post Office. If that's the case, airmail will cost more but will get it there a *lot* faster than surface mail (ship).

I've said that wool wheels don't travel well, but a couple I know managed to bring a wool wheel back from Canada with them on an airplane. They packed the wheel itself in a picture frame crate and packed the rest in their luggage. Now I've heard stories of orchestras traveling by air that had to buy an extra seat ticket for the string base, but I don't think anyone's done this with a spinning wheel . . . yet.

As long as we're on the subject of preventive medicine, let me say a word about children. Anything with moving parts, especially if they can be turned, cranked or pedaled, will have a special fascination for kids. Often they have to see how fast they can make it go, which is not too good for the spinning wheel and leads to things getting broken. Of course, the best prevention is education. Children living in the same house with a spinning wheel, or even visiting often, should be taught to leave it alone. My three-year-old nephew learned this when he was one year old. Or you might try teaching the kids to spin. Kids as young as six or seven can learn if you start them on a drop spindle. The kids you really have to watch out for are the occasional visitors.

There are several things you can do to child-proof a spinning wheel. One method is to take a strong piece of string or cord and tie it around the wheel posts near the base, catching one of the wheel spokes in between (Fig. 11.1). This is a non-damaging, non-permanent way of keeping the wheel from turning. Any spinning wheel on display in a shop should be child-proofed in this manner. Another idea is to take the footman off and hide it.

Fig. 11.1: Child-proofing (immobilizing) a wheel

I told one of my wheel repair customers about these two solutions and she told me, "Oh I don't have to worry about that. I keep my spinning wheel on top of the refrigerator where the kids can't get at it." Well, it *was* a small wheel.

XII
PERSONALITY

As you may have noticed, my first love is for the antique spinning wheels. They have a feeling of history not found with the newly made reproductions. Also, they have a certain something that can only be called "personality".

No two antiques will be the same, even if they were built by the same person. They all wear differently, depending on how they were used, and they will develop their own little idiosyncrasies. The spinning wheel may run beautifully and then suddenly throw its band for no apparent reason. It may uncomplainingly stand up to anything that you can dish out, or it may be fussy and not work at all unless everything is just so. It may run better in one direction than another. It may "talk to you" in a variety of squeaks and creaks and rattles and thumps. The wheel may wobble, the footman may rattle, the wheel may run better some days than others depending on the weather. It all adds up to the fact that each spinning wheel is unique.

A new spinning wheel will have a sort of a personality based on the characteristics of the wheel's style and design, but through use it will acquire a more distinct personality of its own. It takes on something of each person who owns and uses it, and this becomes a part of the spinning wheel.

Who were the people who built and used these spinning wheels? Why were some used more than others? What caused the strange wear pattern on the base of this wheel? Was the red paint on this wheel left over from the barn? Was this very ornate wheel a wedding gift from a bridegroom to his bride? Was it handed down from mother to daughter? How did an East European wheel end up in a North Carolina antique shop? Did it come over to America with an immigrant? Did it come West in a covered wagon? Was it built by an immigrant woodworker who brought with him his pride in good craftsmanship? Was it loved? Only the spinning wheels themselves remain, with a personality that is the sum of their past existence.

POSTSCRIPT

No book is perfect. No author can cover any subject completely enough to satisfy everyone. If you have comments to make on this book, or if you're having troubles with a spinning wheel, drop me a line and I'll try to help. If you're trying to identify a spinning wheel or to describe damage, remember, one picture is worth a thousand words. A clear, close snapshot is a big help.

You can write to me c/o my publisher, or at the following address:

Karen Pauli
513 N. Spring Avenue
LaGrange Park, Illinois 60525

SOURCES (Where To Go For Help)

Here is a listing of where to find many of the things that I have mentioned in this book. It is by no means complete. I tried my best, but I don't know *every* spinning wheel repairman in the country (though I wish I did), and I can't possibly list every modern spinning wheel available or every supplier; that would be a book in itself. I've included what I can and referred you to other sources in some cases. If all else fails, try the reference librarian at your local library.

Spinning Wheel Repairmen/Restorers

I have listed these east to west across the U.S.A. and Canada.

Barbara McManaway. Box 191, Waitsfield, VT 05673, 802-496-4339. Repairs and restores modern and antique wheels. Two to three week wait. Free estimates. Sells antique wheels, specializing in Shaker wheels.

S & C Huber Accoutrements. 82 Plants Dam Rd., East Lyme, Connecticut 06333. 203-739-0772. Repairs and restores modern and antique spinning wheels. Sells antique spinning wheels.

David N. Barrows. 116 86th Street, Virginia Beach, Virginia 23451. 804-428-3250. Repairs and restores modern and antique spinning wheels. Free estimates. Builds modern spinning wheels.

Dan Yeager. Whitehorse Mountain Woodworks, P.O. Box 3023, LaVale, Cumberland, Maryland 21502. Builds the Green Spring Spinning Wheel, usually a two-week wait. Repairs and restores old spinning wheels on a time-and-material basis. Can work from damaged part or accurate drawing, but may occasionally require entire wheel. Free catalog (new spinning wheels and looms).

The Mannings. RD 2, East Berlin, Pennsylvania 17316. 717-624-2223. Spinning instruction, Saxony and Walking Wool wheels, carders, drop spindles, carding machines, distaffs, fibers and dyestuffs, mordants, dyebarks. Special skeined white wool for dyeing. Catalog.

Golden Grain. RR 1, Shelbyville, Michigan 49344. 616-644-4792. Repairs and restores modern and antique spinning wheels. Builds new wheels and looms. Can mail order parts if he has the broken part and the "guzinter" (piece part "goes into"). About one month wait. SASE for catalog (price list) of parts.

R.A. Meisterheim. 32457 Dixon Street, Dowagiac, Michigan 49047. 616-424-5722. Repairs and restores modern and antique spinning wheels. Takes four to six weeks on small items. Free estimates. Builds new wool wheels. Will mail order spinning assemblies and other parts.

Robert Bradley c/o Serendipity Shop, 1523 Ellinwood, Des Plaines, Illinois 60016. 312-297-8094. Will make new parts for antique spinning wheels but will not stain them to match. Will repair broken parts and restore wheels. Great source for spare bobbins. Free estimates.

Lester Lengfeld. 816 Kentucky Ave., Sheboygan, Wisconsin 53081. 414-452-8616. Retired tool and die maker, part-time hobby. Repairs modern and antique spinning wheels. No estimates.

Flintridge Workshop. 121 Woodcrest Rd., Sisters Bay, Wisconsin 54234. 414-854-2919. Repairs and restores modern and antique spinning wheels. No refinishing work done. Work taken on time available basis. Free estimates. Builds and sells spinning wheels. Catalog and price list $.50.

The Old Cabinet Shop. 460 Union St., Box 12, Washingtonville, Ohio 44490. Repairs and restores modern and antique spinning wheels. Waiting list three to four weeks. Free estimates. Can match parts sent by mail, but bring or ship whole wheel is best. Builder of new wheels, winders & accessories. Prices and estimates available.

Arthur L. Johnson. 2502 "C" Street, Lincoln, Nebraska 68502. 477-2096. Restores antique spinning wheels. Custom builds new spinning wheels. Free estimates. One to three month waiting list.

Karl Uhlhorn. Avoca, Nebraska 68307. 402-275-3715. Hobby business. Repairs and restores modern and antique wheels. Six to eight month waiting list. Builds new spinning wheels.

R.G. Walden. General Delivery, Gypsum, Colorado 81637. Full-time wood carver/turner, works on wheels only occasionally. About six weeks wait. Specializes in matching new parts to old wheels. Free estimates. (Author's opinion: sounds like they're quite competent.) Check for cost estimate first. Telephone 303-524-9767.

Alden Amos. c/o Straw Into Gold, 5533 College Ave., Oakland, CA 94618. 415-652-SPIN. Builds textile tools and equipment. Repairs and restorations. Mail-order usually impractical. Waiting list one to three months for repairs, 20 to 30 months for new wheels, looms, etc.

Hungry Hill Homespun. 39918 N. Ruby Lp., Scio, Oregon 97374. 503-394-2731. Part-time business (also raises sheep). Repairs and restores modern and antique wheels. No wait. Free estimates. Will mail order *some* parts.

Ernest L. Mason. 3033 N.E. Davis St., Portland, Oregon 97232. 503-236-3463. Builds new wheels in custom "Shaker Chair" and "Swiss Production" models.

John H. Meehan. 805 N.E. 5th Ave., Camas, Washington 98607. 206-834-5525. Restores antiques. Specializes in matching parts. No mail order. Free estimates if wheel is brought in. (Author's opinion: sounds quite competent.)

C & G Rognvaldson. RR 4, Acton, Ontario, Canada L7J 2M1. 519-853-0249. Repairs wheels. Can repair or duplicate broken parts by mail, but prefers to have the whole spinning wheel. Free estimates. Builds new upright wheels (old family business).

Ye Olde Spinning Wheel. Alfred Colbeck, RR 5, Bolton, Ontario, Canada L0P 1A0. 416-857-1357. Repairs and restores modern and antique wheels. Will mail order some parts. Free estimates. Builds new spinning wheels.

Eliza Leadbeater. Rookery Cottage, Dalefords Lane, Whitegate, Northwich, Cheshire, England CW8 2BN Telephone 060/882879. Restores antique spinning wheels. Few days' wait; 48 hours for bobbin and flyer. Free estimates and information. Restores and sells antique Scandinavian spinning wheels. Builds new wheels. Visitors by appointment.

Spinning Wheel Plans

Books and Magazines

Foxfire Book II. Elliot Wigginton, ed. Anchor/Doubleday, pub. Garden City, New York. ©1973. Contains information and diagrams for building a wool wheel, primitive yarn winder and barn loom. Also contains information on "olden times" spinning and weaving.

Popular Mechanic's Do-It-Yourself Encyclopedia. Vol. 13, pp. 2435-2439. Book Division, Hearst Magazines, New York, New York 10019. ©1968. Collected articles from *Popular Mechanic's* magazine. If you can't get access to the *Encyclopedia*, try writing the magazine for a copy of the article. The plans are for an upright or parlor wheel. The blueprints are complete and accurate, but the story of the wheel's origin is highly unlikely.

Shuttle, Spindle, and Dyepot. Put out by the Handweaver's Guild of America. 65 LaSalle Rd., P.O. Box 7-374, West Hartford, Connecticut 06107. This magazine occasionally prints plans and information on building spinning and weaving equipment or adapting and improving existing equipment. Some reprints available at member/nonmember prices. Drop spindle plans $1.00/$1.50. Modern Tyrolean wheel plans $3.00/$4.50.

Workbench Magazine. Modern Handicrafts, Inc. 4251 Pennsylvania, Kansas City, Missouri 64111. This magazine has printed plans for two spinning wheels and a yarn winder. Copies of the plans are available for the cost of a photostat. Upright wheel plans, Jan./Feb. 1972 issue. Saxony wheel plans, March/April and May/June 1967 issues. Yarn winder (clock reel), Jan./Feb. 1971 issue. $1.50 each.

Mailorder

Craftplans Company. 21801 Industrial Blvd., Rogers, Minnesota 55374. Catalog $.50. Vertical (upright) spinning wheel plans, #403. Colonial (Saxony) spinning wheel plans, #379. Pennsylvania Dutch wool wheel plans, #404. Four-harness loom plans, #396. $2.25 each.

Furniture Designs. 1425 Sherman Ave., Evanston, Illinois 60201. Catalog $1, refundable with first order. Full-sized plans. $.25 postage and handling for each set of plans. #181—Saxony spinning wheel $8.00. #182—Large Saxony spinning wheel $10.00.

Woodcraft Supply Corporation. 313 Montvale Ave., Woburn, Massachusetts 01888. All plans $11.75 postpaid. Welsh Saxony wheel plans. English upright plans. Norwegian wheel plans.

Spinning & Weaving Suppliers

It would be impossible to list all of these! The shops that I usually deal with are:

Serendipity Shop. 1523 Ellinwood, Des Plaines, Illinois 60016. 312-297-8094. This shop carries most of the books that I refer to and a wide selection of spinning and weaving supplies. They will also mail order. Catalog $1.00.

Boll Weavel's. 22 West Chicago Ave., Naperville, Illinois 60540. Small but growing. They carry a nice selection of spinning and weaving supplies. No catalog yet.

The Wool Works. 1812 N. Farwell Ave., Milwaukee, WI 53202.

For other suppliers, I refer you to:

Supplier's Directory: Shuttle, Spindle, and Dyepot magazine. 65 LaSalle Road, P.O. Box 7-374, West Hartford, Connecticut 06107. This is a comprehensive directory of spinning and weaving suppliers in the U.S., Canada and around the world listed by location. It's available from the magazine for $3.00 ($3.50 foreign) for subscribers and $4.50 for non-subscribers. Well worth the price.

Shuttle, Spindle, and Dyepot magazine (see address above). Publishes quarterly. $4.25 per copy; subscription $15.00 per year, $42.00 for three years. Foreign subscribers add $2.00 per year. This magazine has a regular "test and report" column as well as a good deal of advertising by spinning and weaving suppliers. Sometimes available at larger public libraries and university libraries.

Handwoven. Interweave Press, Inc., 306 North Washington Ave., Loveland, Colorado 80537. Publishes 5 times a year. $15.00 for 1 year, $27.50 for 2 years. $18.75 per year Canada and overseas, surface delivery. U.S. funds only. Available over-the-counter at many weaving shops. A very good spinning and weaving magazine. Contains many advertisements from spinning and weaving suppliers.

Spin·Off. Published yearly by Interweave Press (see address above). $5.50 per copy. The only magazine I know of devoted exclusively to spinning. Covers all phases of spinning and has a lot of good information on spinning wheels. Many ads by suppliers.

Books

The following, plus the above publications, constitute my reference library.

Spinning Wheels, The John Horner Collection. Compiled by G.B. Thompson, O.B.E. M.Sc., F.M.A. Published by the Ulster Museum, Belfast, Northern Ireland. Reprinted July, 1976. Paperback $1.50. A catalog of the Ulster Museum's collection of spinning wheels. A good reference book for identifying European spinning wheels.

A Pictorial Guide to American Spinning Wheels. David Pennington and Michael Taylor. Published by Shaker Press, Sabbathday Lake, Poland Spring, Maine 04274. ©1975. Paperback $4.50. An excellent directory to American spinning wheels and some of their European ancestors. Includes early American patent wheels. Good clear photographs and explanations.

Spinning and Weaving With Wool. Paula Simmons. Published by Pacific Search Press, 222 Dexter Ave. N., Seattle, Washington 98109. ©1977. Paperback $12.95 ($16.95 in Canada). A very good book showing all phases of preparing, spinning and weaving wool. It also has a chapter that is a catalog of modern spinning wheels available today.

Handspindles. Bette Hochberg, 333 Wilkes Circle, Santa Cruz, California 95060. Paperback $5.95 ($6.50 postpaid for mail order). Reviews and illustrates ethnic spindles through history and around the world, and how to use them.

Alden Amos's Spinning Wheel Primer. Alden Amos. Published by Straw Into Gold, 5533 College Ave., Oakland, California 94618. ©1976. Paperback. Analysis of different types of spinning wheels and their advantages, disadvantages and size and whorls or drive ratios. A little technical, but good.

A Reverence For Wood. Eric Sloane. Hardcover published by Funk and Wagnals, 10 E. 53rd, New York, New York 10022; $12.95. Paperback published by Random House, 201 E. 50th, New York, New York under a Ballantine title; $4.95. Not a book on spinning wheels, but a wonderful volume on early American woodworking. Helps you understand and appreciate the construction of antique spinning wheels.

The Joy of Spinning. Marilyn Kluger. Published by Simon and Schuster, Rockefeller Center, 630 Fifth Ave., New York, New York 10020. ©1971. Hardcover $6.95. Paperback $4.95. This was my teacher. Clearly written to easily learn from. Her anecdotes and folklore make it very enjoyable reading.

Your Handspinning. Elsie G. Davenport. Select Books, 5969 Wilbur Ave., Tarzana, CA 0356. $5.00.